Dear ,

" May the Lamb
that was slain
receive the reward ,
of His sufferings. '

Love Julia

Sermons on

The Lord's Supper

by

Jonathan Edwards

Compiled and Edited by
Dr. Don Kistler

The Northampton Press

The Northampton Press
P.O. Box 781135, Orlando, FL 32878-1135
www.northamptonpress.org

*

*

ISBN 0-9798579-0-2

*

Library of Congress Control Number: 20079905892

*

Special thanks to the Jonathan Edwards Center at Yale University for
making these sermons available for publication.

This book has been made possible by the generosity of
Mr. Charles deAndrade.

Contents

Appendix

1

The Thing Designed in the Sacrament of the Lord's Supper Is the Communion of Christians in the Body and Blood of Christ

"The cup of blessing which we bless, is it not the communion of the blood of Christ? The bread which we break, is it not the communion of the body of Christ?"
1 Corinthians 10:16

The scope of the apostle from the beginning of chapter 8 to the end of chapter 10 seems to be to dissuade the Corinthian Christians from eating things offered to idols. The case with those who were converted to Christianity in Corinth was this: they dwelt among the heathen who made up the far greater part of the city. And the heathen inhabitants were wont publicly to celebrate festivals in honor to their gods, which were times of feasting and mirth among them; they were wont to invite their friends to those feasts where they ate things sacrificed to idols.

So the Christians who were scattered about among them by this means had a notable temptation laid before

them, for their heathen relations and acquaintances
would sometimes invite them to their feasts. And there
were some among them who pleaded for the lawfulness of
going and eating things offered to idols at such feasts.
They argued that it was a part of their Christian liberty,
and that, since the Ceremonial Law was abrogated, all
things that were fit now for the body were lawful to be
eaten, that having been offered to idols did not change its
nature to make it unclean, and that the scrupling of it was
a needless and ignorant scruple.

But the apostle argues in chapter 8 that it is not fitting
in such cases to eat meats offered to idols for the sake of
others who see them because it will be a visible worship-
ping of idols. If they see 'em at feasts eating things offered
to idols, they won't know nor have opportunity to know
but that they eat it as offered to idols and with conscience
of the idol as the heathen do—and so the Christian name
will be greatly dishonored, and their weak brethren may
be drawn by their example to do the like against their consciences. And the apostle tells 'em that, rather than make
a brother to offend, he would eat no meat while the world
stands.

And that they might not think it hard to put themselves
so much out of their way for the sake of their brethren, he
tells 'em in chapter 9 how much he denied himself of lawful liberties for the sake of others in much greater instances than not eating things offered to idols, in refrain-
ing from marriage, in taking no wages for his labor in the
ministry, which he might challenge if he would, in becoming to the Jews as a Jew.

In the beginning of this chapter the apostle uses another argument to dissuade them from it, taken from the accounts that the Old Testament gives of the dreadful judgments of God against idolaters amongst the Israelites in the wilderness.

And here, in this part of the chapter wherein is our text, he begins another argument. He shows that eating things that are known by them, and by others who see them, to be things offered to idols is a visible joining in the worship of idols from a parallel drawn between the Holy Supper of the Christians and the Mosaic sacrifices of the Israelites and the sacrifices of the heathens.

The apostle's argument is this: as it was among the Israelites, they who ate of the sacrifices visibly joined in the worship of the altar, as in verse 18: "Behold Israel after the flesh are not they which eat of the sacrifices, partakers of the altar, and as those that sat eating and drinking together at the Lord's Table, they were all looked upon to have communion or to be partakers in the worship of Christ, as in our text. So they who were seen eating things that were known to be offered to idols had visible communion or fellowship in the worship of devils, as the apostle infers in the conclusion in verses 19–21.

Therefore, that is what is aimed at in the text, that those who eat things that are known to be offered to idols do visibly join or have communion in the worship of devils in the same manner as all who partake of the elements of bread and wine in the Lord's Supper have visible communion in the worship of Christ.

"The cup of blessing which we bless, is it not the communion of the blood of Christ?" that is, when we drink of the cup after it has been blessed in the name of Christ, have we not thereby visible communion in the blood of Christ? For the blessing of the bread and wine in this case is parallel to the ceremony of offering of beasts in heathen sacrifices. And therefore the heathen priest's offering renders the eating after that a having visible fellowship with devils as the Christian minister's blessing of the bread and wine renders the eating after that a having a visible fellowship in or communion in the body and blood of Christ.

DOCTRINE: The thing designed in the sacrament of the Lord's Supper is the communion of Christians in the body and blood of Christ.

1. What it is to have communion in the body and blood of Christ.

2. How this is the design of the sacrament of the Lord's Supper.

1. What it is to have communion in the body and blood of Christ. The word "communion" denotes the common partaking in union of any good. Whatsoever any two or more partake of together or in society, that they have communion in. In order, therefore, to fully answer this inquiry, it may be divided into two inquiries: what is meant by communion or partaking of the body and blood of Christ, and who this communion or common participation is with. For in communion there is to be considered the common good that is partaken of and the persons who are partaken with, or who are united in this partaking.

First, we will inquire what is intended by the partaking of the body and blood of Christ that is designed in the

Lord's Supper, for there is no such thing as our partaking of the body and blood of Christ in a proper sense. The end of the sacrament is not that we may eat the flesh and drink the blood of Christ without a metaphor. And if we should suggest a thing so horrid and so monstrous as the papists do in their doctrine of transubstantiation, would that be any benefit to us? And though Christ said when He administered the first sacrament of the body, "This is My body," and of the wine, "This is My blood," yet there is no more reason to understand the words in a proper sense than that we should understand the words of David when he longed for the water of the well of Bethlehem and three mighty men broke through the host of the Philistines and brought some of it; and he, refusing to drink it, poured it out and said, "This is the blood of the men that went in jeopardy of their lives" (2 Samuel 23:17). It is as reasonable to suppose that David meant that the water was really and in a proper sense the blood that ran in the veins of those three mighty men as that Christ, when He said of the wine in the sacrament, "This is My blood," meant that it was strictly and properly His blood.

It is not that therefore that is the design of the sacrament, that we might be partakers of Christ's body and blood in strictness of speech. But these two things are intended: Our partaking of the benefits that are procured by Christ's body and blood. Our soul's partaking of these spiritual benefits is represented by partaking of the body and blood of Christ itself because those benefits are well compared to food; they are the food and nourishment and life of our souls, which we could not obtain in any other way than by Christ's being slain. It was as necessary that Christ should be slain, His body broken and blood spilt, in order to our souls being fed and nourished with spiritual food, as it is that beasts should be slain in order to our eating their flesh.

Therefore the case is thus figuratively well represented in Scripture that the soul of man is naturally destitute of its necessary food; it is ready to perish with famine, and must unavoidably perish unless our spiritual food is given to us, which food is the Lord Jesus Christ. There is nothing else that will supply our wants, no other food that will nourish, renew, and satisfy our souls that are reduced to such a perishing condition by our spiritual famine. John 6:53: "Except ye eat the flesh of the Son of man and drink His blood ye have no life in you." And we can't have Christ for our food unless He is slain for us.

Such therefore was Christ's great love to us that He yielded and was willing to be slain and distributed amongst us so that we might live, and that a blessed feast might be prepared for our souls. John 6:51: "And the bread which I will give is My flesh, which I will give for the life of the world."

This was signified by the sacrifices of old, and especially by the Paschal Lamb. The innocent lamb must be slain before they could eat him and so keep the feast upon him.

Our partaking of the benefits that are procured by the sacrifice of Christ's body and blood is rather compared to eating His body and blood also because it is by faith in that body and blood, or in that Sacrifice, receiving it and applying it to ourselves and depending upon it that we receive those benefits. This faith and dependence on the body and blood for the benefits is, as it were, eating and drinking His body and blood in order to receive satisfaction and nourishment.

Therefore by our having communion in the body and blood of Christ is signified our partaking of all gospel benefits, the pardon of sin and being received into God's favor, being made God's children, being sanctified, receiving God's image and, after being received to eternal life and blessedness—for all these are the purchase of the sacrifice of Christ's body and blood.

By our partaking of Christ's body and blood, our having blessedness in the person of Christ, Christ's body and blood have been offered in sacrifice to procure happiness for us. And this happiness is in having our souls united to His person in beholding His excellencies and glory, and in the enjoyment of His love in having spiritual conversation with Him in this world, and in enjoying Him in the world to come.

Believers live upon Christ in this sense, that the excellencies of the Person of Christ and His love are their food. Christ is their treasure. He is their Pearl of Great Price. Having communion in the body and blood of Christ therefore implies our having happiness in spiritually beholding and feeding upon the glories and beauties of His Person and His marvelous love and complacence in us, which we also come to by the sacrifice of His body and blood.

But it remains, second, to be inquired who Christians have communion with in this, or who they partake with of these blessings.

(1) They therein have communion with Christ; they not only have communion in Him, but they have commun-

ion with Him. They not only partake of Him but they are joint partakers with Him. The Head and members partake together of the same life and health.

The father and children in a family partake of the same food; so, when Christ invites His people to the gospel feast, He sits with them at the table.

Christ, as Mediator and Surety, partakes with His people of the benefits of His own body and blood, of the benefits of His own sacrifice and righteousness. He has justification from imputed sin by His death. He becoming our Surety, our iniquities were laid upon Him. He was made sin for us. He had our guilt laid upon Him, and thereby stood obliged to suffer the penalty of the Law; but by His suffering He was freed from this guilt. And when God the Father released Him from the prison of the grave, then He was justified, as having suffered enough to answer the imputed guilt that lay upon Him.

So He is rewarded for His own obedience, of which the offering up of His body and blood was the greatest act. Because He made His soul an offering for sin, therefore God has given Him a portion with the great. "He became obedient unto death; therefore hath God highly exalted Him" (Philippians 2:8–9).

So that believers, in their being justified from sin by Christ's death and having eternal life by His obedience, have fellowship with Christ in His own sacrifice. And therefore Christ, in the first sacrament, partook Himself with His disciples of that bread and wine that signified His own body and blood that He gave to them. And so He still partakes with His children in the spiritual benefits signified in the Lord's Supper. And He, by His bodily presence at the first sacrament, would signify that He ever more will be with those who in a holy manner attend on that ordinance, and they may look upon Him as sitting with them at His table.

They have communion with the rest who sit down with them at the Lord's Table; they partake with them of the same spiritual benefits of the sacrifice of Christ's body and blood, and of the same blessedness in the Person of Jesus Christ. It may be that many of those who sit down do not partake of those spiritual benefits, but this is designed in the Lord's Supper, that those who sit together should, as one society or family, feast upon their spiritual food; for we are all partakers of that one bread.

(2) They have communion with the universal church throughout the whole world. They all are united in the same Head; all are partakers of the same spiritual blessings, of the same spiritual food, the same body and blood of Christ. And this communion is designed in the sacrament of the Lord's Supper. See the verse following the text. 1 Corinthians 10:17: "For we being many are one bread and one body, for we are all partakers of that one bread." All the church of Christ has communion together in spiritual benefits. 1 Corinthians 12:12–13: "For as the body is one and hath many members, and all the members of that one body being many are one body, so also is Christ; for by one spirit we are all baptized into one body, whether we be Jews or Gentiles, bond or free, and have been all made to drink into one Spirit." And Ephesians 4:4–6: "There is one body and one Spirit, even as ye are called in one hope, one Lord, one faith, one baptism, one God and Father of us all."

(3) Lastly, there is designed in the sacrament of the Lord's Supper communion with the church triumphant in heaven. The happiness that they have in glory is in Scripture compared to a feast that God has prepared for them; 'tis the marriage supper of the Lamb, and that which they feast on there is the body and blood of Christ, that is, they are spiritual blessings purchased by the sacrifice of His body and blood. They live upon the glory and love of Christ. There they enjoy those blessings in abundance; they eat and drink abundantly, even to their full satisfaction.

The Lord's Supper therefore is designed that the church on earth might have communion with the church in heaven, that they might be partakers of the same spiritual food in a lesser degree here in this world, and that they might by means of it be brought to the same perfection. All the true members of Christ's church here have communion with the church in glory in God's ordinances. Hebrews 12:22: "That ye are come to Mt. Zion."

2. The second inquiry is how the communion of the body and blood of Christ is designed in the sacrament of the Lord's Supper. And that is in these two ways, that is, as this communion is hereby signified and sealed.

First, our communion of the body and blood of Christ is hereby signified or by sensible signs represented. God has in Christ Jesus prepared a glorious feast for the poor, needy souls of His chosen ones; and He has been pleased to appoint an outward feast to be observed in His church in all ages to represent it here.

The body and blood of Christ and the benefits we receive by them are here represented by the sacramental elements of bread and wine, which are chosen with admirable wisdom for this end. The use of these is much more agreeable to the gospel dispensation than if the flesh and blood of beasts had been appointed for this end. The use of flesh in holy things was abrogated upon the abrogation of legal sacrifices.

They are much more agreeable to the simplicity of the gospel of Christ than if some pompous feast with a variety of dainties had been appointed for this end. Christ, in the institution of the gospel, has purposely avoided all ceremonial pomp. These elements do most fitly represent the body and blood of Christ with respect to the benefits we receive by them. Bread, which is food that is more universally used as such than perhaps any other kind of thing, and is of a very wholesome, nourishing, strengthening nature (Psalm 104:15), is often in Scripture put for food in general. It fitly represents the spiritual strength and nourishment that we receive of Christ, from whom we receive the life of our souls, and the preservation, establishment, and perfection of that life.

Wine very fitly represents that spiritual life, vigor, refreshment and joy that are to be had in Christ and that He has purchased for us by His blood. It well signifies that rest that the weary and heavy-laden with sin have when they come to Christ, having the guilt of sin cleansed by His blood. Proverbs 31:6: "Give wine to him that is of a heavy heart." It fitly represents the spiritual joy that believers have in Christ's beauty and love. Psalm 104:15: "And wine that maketh glad men's heart."

These benefits are often compared to bread and wine in the Old Testament. Psalm 132:15: "I will satisfy her poor

with bread." Isaiah 33:16: "He shall dwell on high; his place
of defense shall be the munitions of rocks. Bread shall be
given him." Isaiah 25:6: "And on this mountain shall the
Lord of hosts make unto all people a feast of fat things of
wines on the lees." Isaiah 55:1: "Ho, every one that
thirsteth, come ye to the waters, and he that hath no
money; come ye, buy, and eat; yea, come, buy wine and
milk without money and without price."

Bread and wine were also under the Old Testament
used as types of that spiritual nourishment that we receive
of Christ. There was the showbread of the temple and the
unleavened bread of the Passover; they signified the same
thing as bread in the sacrament. Bread, corn, and wine
were the meat and drink offering that were offered with
their sacrifices and signified the body and blood of Christ.
It was bread and wine that Melchizedek, the priest of the
Most High God who represented Christ, brought forth to
Abraham, the father of the faithful, when he blessed him
returning from the slaughter of the kings (Genesis 14:18).
This typified Christ offering His body and blood, or the
benefits thereof, to believers.

In this ordinance is represented the way in which we
come to have communion or to be partakers of this body
and blood of Christ and the benefits thereof, both in what
is done on Christ's part and what is done on our part.

Here is represented what is done on Christ's part in
order to our being made partakers of His body and blood.
Particularly, here is represented Christ's offering Himself
up as a sacrifice for us in the bruising of His body and spilling His blood by the breaking of the bread and the pouring out of the wine. Galatians 3:1: "O foolish Galatians,

who hath bewitched you, that ye should not obey the truth, before whose eyes Jesus Christ hath been evidently set forth, crucified among you?"

Indeed, hereby are not merely signified His outward sufferings, but the whole of His passion; for by the shedding of His blood and the bruising of His body are meant by a synecdoche of the part for the whole, not only His sufferings in His body, but also in His soul those agonies and that sorrow which He felt there. His internal sufferings could not be represented by outward signs, and therefore only the outward part is put for the whole.

The bread is broken all in pieces, which signifies more than what was done to Christ's body when He was crucified; it signifies the greatness and extremity of His sufferings: He was, as it were, broken in pieces for us. It is by Christ thus suffering for us that way is made for our communion of the benefits of the gospel. Christ died for us that we might have eternal life in Him.

It is the will of God that this wonderful and marvelous act of Christ, yielding Himself to die and offering Himself up in sacrifice for us, should be commemorated in the church in all ages by this representation of it in this ordinance. We are to do it according to the institution in remembrance of Christ, and especially in remembrance of His death. 1 Corinthians 11:26: "for as often as ye eat this bread and drink this cup, ye do show the Lord's death till He come."

In this ordinance is represented Christ offering His body and blood to us and bestowing the same upon us in its being offered and given to the church by the minister who here stands in Christ's stead and represents Him. He gives the sacramental elements to the people in the name of Christ.

The same offer that Christ makes of Himself and His benefits in the gospel is here made in offering those elements that are signs of those benefits. Here is shown how we wholly depend upon Christ: we live upon Him as our spiritual food in that what we here eat and drink represents Him; and not only so, but it is He who offers, and He bestows upon us this meat and drink. Though His body is broken and His blood spilt, yet we shall be never the better for it unless He bestows it upon us.

In this ordinance is represented what is done on our part in order to our communion of gospel benefits purchased by His body and blood, that is, our receiving and feeding on Christ by faith by receiving, eating, and drinking the bread and wine.

'Tis by faith that we accept Christ's offer of Himself and benefits; 'tis by faith that we are united to Christ and live upon Him; 'tis by faith that we come to have actual communion in the body and blood of Christ. Nothing else is required on our part but only taking and eating. We have it as freely as those who are freely invited to a feast have their food only for taking and eating of it.

In this ordinance is represented the saints' actual enjoyment of communion in Christ's body and blood and their blessedness therein. A feast denotes joy; they are generally made upon joyful occasions. This feast denotes the saints' happiness in the enjoyment of Christ, and that mutual joy there is between Him and believer in their common participation.

Wine signifies the happiness of heaven. Matthew 26:29:

"But I say unto you, I will not drink henceforth of this fruit of the vine, until that day when I drink it new with you in my Father's kingdom." 1 Corinthians 10:16: "The cup of blessing which we bless, is it not the communion of the blood of Christ? The bread which we break, is it not the communion of the body of Christ?"

Thus is our communion of the body and blood of Christ represented or signified in this ordinance of the Lord's Supper.

Second, our communion in the body and blood of Christ is hereby sealed; that is, the covenant of grace, by virtue of which it is that we come to be partakers of Christ's body and blood, or of the benefits of the gospel, is sealed hereby. And the seal that is here given is both on God's part and on our part. God sets His own seal to the covenant of grace, and we also set our seal. We seal our own engagements.

In this ordinance, God seals to us our communion in the benefits of the gospel. This ordinance is appointed for this end not only to represent those benefits, but to signify the certainty of our obtaining 'em if we will accept them as offered in the gospel. We have God's promises in the gospel, and there are those sensible actions that God has appointed to be added to the promises to signify the same thing, to certify in God's name the fulfillment of them.

These actions of breaking the bread and pouring out the wine, and giving them to the people are, as it were, a visible promise that upon our accepting the things signified by them at the hands of Christ we shall enjoy them; and the actions and signs signify the same to the eye as the promises do to the ear.

It being done for this end by God's appointment and by His authority in His name, 'tis as much as if God expressly renewed His promise every time that we receive the sacrament. Those words, "This is My body" and "this is the cup of the New Testament," imply a promise.

'Tis a seal on our part as God in this ordinance seals His covenant to us so we, by attending on the ordinance and by receiving Christ's body and blood, do openly own and renew the covenant of grace. We seal our engagements to be the Lord's; we do in the most solemn manner give ourselves up to God to be His in an everlasting covenant and to cleave to Him and to His people.

This is one thing that is the language of these actions of ours that we perform at the table of the Lord: by taking the bread and wine we do profess to take Christ for our Portion, to take Him as the proper nourishment and refreshment of our souls, to take Him as He whom we will live upon as being sufficient to satisfy our hungry and thirsty souls, and so to renounce the vanities of this world.

We take Him as our only and all-sufficient Savior and Redeemer, professing our dependence alone on His body and blood for life, renouncing our dependence on all our own righteousness. We take Him as our Lord and King, and give ourselves up to His government, renouncing all ways of sin. And as we here have communion with the church, with those we partake with, and with the universal church, so we here seal our engagements to live and walk towards them as members of the same body, as children of the same family.

As there is in this ordinance a profession of faith and love towards the Lord Jesus Christ, so there is likewise a profession of love for those who are His. The sacrament is a feast of charity. Other feasts do betoken mutual friendship and good understanding in the guests; so more especially does this feast express and seal Christian love and charity among the disciples of Christ. Feasts were used of old, and still are, as seals of peace, as between Isaac and Abimelech (Genesis 26:30).

And thus we may understand something of the nature and design of this holy ordinance of the Lord's Supper, and it appears by what has been said that the same things are in this ordinance exhibited to our eyes that are in the Word to our ears. We have in this sacrament the sum of the gospel in sensible signs.

Here we have shown us how Christ died and suffered for our sake. Here it is shown what those sufferings were for, for the spiritual life, nourishment, strength, joy, and happiness of our souls. Here we have the offers of the gospel made to us; the covenant is here declared by sensible signs, that if we will receive Jesus Christ by faith we shall be partakers of all the benefits that Christ has purchased; and we are here taught that Christ alone is the Bestower of these benefits. We here have shown and represented to us the blessedness of those who comply with the gospel in that the feast of spiritual and heavenly delights and joys is here represented by this outward feast.

Here also we have the promises of the gospel in sensible signs, the same things ascertained to us by those signs that are for the promises of the gospel. Here likewise our gospel duty towards those who are Christ's is represented, engaged and sealed.

Therefore this sacrament is a means of our partaking

of the benefits of the gospel after the same manner as the preaching of the gospel is; for in one we have the gospel set before us in words, and in the other we have it in signs. Indeed, there is something further in this ordinance than in preaching the gospel, because the promises of the gospel are here after a more solemn manner renewed and sealed on God's part, and the covenant is also owned and our engagements sealed on our part. But the sum of what is aimed at in it, next to the honor and glory of Christ, is our communion with Christ and with His people in the benefits purchased by Christ.

Application

USE OF INFORMATION. This may lead us to take notice of God's great goodness in thus making provision for our souls. It should lead us to admire God's grace in providing such a spiritual feast for us as this which is here outwardly represented and designed, that He should have such love for us as to provide food for our life and refreshment at such great cost; that He would give us the flesh and blood of His own Son for our meat and drink.

The food is the richest and most rare kind, unto which that which is served up at princes' tables is not to be compared; it is the fruit of the tree of life that grows in the midst of the paradise of God and the water of the river of life, the river of God's pleasures. We are fed with angels' food, the true bread from heaven signified by the manna in the wilderness. So great is the goodness of God to men that men may eat angels' food (Psalm 78:25).

This food is such as we were in necessity of; our souls

would surely perish without it. And so rich and excellent is
it that it could not be gotten for gold; neither might silver
be weighed for the price thereof. All the treasures of this
world would not be sufficient to purchase it. It was therefore bought at a vastly dearer rate, even with no less than
the precious blood of the eternal Son of God.

What kind of mercy is this, that God should make such
provision for such poor creatures as we are. We aren't
those who are worthy to be so treated. We were not great,
rich, excellent, and honorable; but we were some of those
spoken of who were invited to the great supper. Luke
14:21: "Bring in hither the poor, the maimed, the halt, and
the blind." We were a poor, base, wretched company before Christ called us in hither to this feast. We were found
in the highways and hedges as poor, wandering, lost creatures without house or home, without food or clothing.

But what a difference is made in their state whom
Christ has brought to the gospel feast. He has washed
them in His own blood. He has healed their wounds. He
has taken away their filthy garments and clothed them in
princely robes; and now they feast and fare better than
kings in their earthly palaces.

Such provision as this is made for us and is offered to
all of us. And God uses abundant means to bring us to
partake of it. We have the call of God in the written Word
and, besides, His appointed ambassadors to set before us
the gospel provision and, in Christ's stead, to beseech us,
as it were, to compel us to come and eat. Not only so, but
we have these glorious blessings and the way wherein they
may be made ours set as before our eyes in this ordinance,
together with the promise of God sealed that if we will

come we shall be accepted and shall be blessed in communion with Christ.

God greatly condescends to us in providing such a variety of means, and in so suiting means to our present state and nature. God considers that we are made up of body and soul, and that, in our present state of union with our bodies, we are apt to be affected with what is the object of our senses. So that God has, as it were, made the gospel visible in this ordinance. He has in visible signs set before our eyes what we in the gospel hear with our ears.

God has exercised a marvelous wisdom in contriving this ordinance for our benefit in the choice He has made of the elements or materials, and in His ordering the actions that belong to it, which are so very significant and so agreeable to the gospel dispensation.

USE OF REPROOF. Let this reprove those who neglect to come to the Lord's Supper. If our communion in and partaking of the blessings purchased by Christ's body and blood are the design of it; if it is appointed as a great means of this—then those who neglect coming to this ordinance are guilty of casting a visible contempt upon the body and blood of Christ.

They say they don't do it from contempt, but that is the language of it; neglecting the ordinance of the Lord's Supper is as much a visible contempt cast upon Him as the attendance on any duty of worship is a visible honor done to Him.

The apostle in our context exhorts the Christians not to eat things offered to idols because it was a visible worship of those idols, and he would have them not only in their hearts, but openly to cast off idols by abstaining from eating things offered to them. So, for the same reason, neglecting the Lord's Supper is a visible rejecting and casting off of Jesus Christ. Forsaking the heathen temples, sacrifices, and heathen festivals was a visible renouncing of heathenism; so forsaking or shunning this Christian feast is a visible renunciation of Christianity.

Herein consists a main part of outward or visible religion, in attending on outward ordinances of worship. Therefore, in rejecting the ordinances of the Christian religion, we do so far cast off the visibility of the Christian religion.

The sacrament of the Lord's Supper is one of the greatest of Christian ordinances; and it is more distinguishing than other ordinances, except baptism. One end of these two ordinances is to distinguish those who are of the visible church as visible Christians from the rest of the world. As for public prayers and preaching, a heathen may come in and be present at them to satisfy his curiosity; they are not so distinguishing, and, therefore, the visibility of Christianity does not consist so much in them.

They therefore who call themselves Christians and turn their backs upon the Lord's Supper act inconsistently with themselves; they make a profession of religion in some things, but as openly reject it in others.

There was not in the primitive times of the church such a neglect of this ordinance amongst professing Christians as is nowadays, particularly amongst the Christian Corinthians, as those who professed the religion of Christ generally commemorated His death, as is evident by our context; for doubtless, when the apostle dehorts them from eating things sacrificed to idols, he speaks to them all in general and he uses this as one argument with them: it did not become those who partook of the Lord's Supper. 1 Corinthians 10:21: "Ye cannot drink of the cup of the Lord and of the cup of devils; ye cannot be partakers of the Lord's Table and of the table of devils." That was the way in those days: those who were professing Christians partook of the Lord's Table and those who were heathens partook of the idol's table—and by that, heathens and Christians might be distinguished one from another.

This attendance on the Lord's Supper is a very known duty of Christianity; we have very express and positive commands to attend the same. And doubtless it must be very displeasing to Him to see it so much neglected, no less than the stated neglect of other duties of religion. And such as live in neglect of it, how can they expect God's blessing upon their soul when they do not seek God in all the ways of His institution? God of old directed His people to wait upon Him at His altar, and there to expect His blessing. Exodus 20:24: "An altar of earth shalt thou make unto Me and shalt sacrifice thereon thy burnt offerings, thy sheep and thine oxen in all places where I record My name. There I will come unto thee and I will bless thee." The same may be said of the communion table in the New Testament. They were in the way of a blessing in coming to the altar, and so will Christians be when they come to the Lord's Supper.

OBJECTION. But many excuse themselves and quiet their consciences by saying they aren't prepared to come, and it is not their duty to come when they are not prepared.

ANSWER 1. All those who make this excuse don't do it

in sincerity. They excuse themselves with this, but this is not the true reason. But they indeed have no desirousness of coming, neither from any love to gospel ordinances nor from any concern for their souls. Their concern for their souls is not great enough to bring them here as appears by their neglect of other appointed duties. They don't wait upon God in other ways of His appointment. There are many of them who neglect secret prayer; they do that because they think they aren't prepared. For then why do they come to meetings and are present at public prayers?

There are many of them who neglect the Lord's Supper for the same reasons as they neglect prayer, reading the Scriptures, and giving attention at meetings, from a stupid neglect of their souls and an aversion to holy things.

They don't love to be concerned with religion; they have no relish for it, nor yet have they that concern for their souls that they are willing to seek God in all ways that it is their duty to do it in.

ANSWER 2. But if that isn't the case with you, and you are really so concerned that you are willing to do anything for your soul's good, you can do those things to prepare yourself so that you will be in your way to come. If you live in a way of known wickedness and intend to live in one still, I acknowledge that you are not fit to come. If you do so come, you'll eat and drink damnation to yourself. But if you are so concerned for your soul as has been supposed, you can forsake all known sin and you can perform all external known duties. You can set apart a suitable time to meditate on the nature and ends of the ordinance, and by reading and prayer fit yourself for it. And you can come to the sacrament for a religion end, viz., the good of your soul, with a serious and real intention of improving it and all other ordinances with your utmost diligence.

ANSWER 3. If you aren't willing to be at the self-denial and pains of doing thus, then don't think that you bring less guilt upon you for not attending the Lord's Supper. If you don't come to the ordinance because you aren't prepared, and aren't prepared because you won't be prepared, and because you choose rather to be unprepared, your unpreparedness won't lighten your punishment for your neglect of your duty.

If God commands you to come to His table, but bids you prepare yourself first, you won't have the less to suffer for not coming at His call because you would not be at the pains and self-denial of preparation.

Are you going on in a way of drunkenness or a way of uncleanness? 'Tis true, you aren't fit to come to the Lord's Supper. But don't make that an excuse, that you are a drunkard and are lascivious, and so don't come. For why don't you leave off your drunkenness and uncleanness and come? Your punishment for abstaining won't be the less for your willfully unfitting yourself.

USE OF EXHORTATION. Let this exhort you to prepare for the sacrament of the Lord's Supper that you may have the communion of Christ's body and blood in it. There is that sacredness and solemnity belonging to this that it is a very dreadful thing to come to it in a careless and profane manner. It is most sacred by reason of those most sacred things represented in it. We have, as it were, in this ordinance Christ crucified among us and for us. Here we see that great and wonderful thing, as it were, transacted, the death of the Son of God. Therefore, those who come in a regardless manner, as though they were going to sit down at their own tables to take their ordinary food not only miss the benefit designed in the ordinance, communion of the benefits of the gospel we have been speaking of, but they render themselves guilty of the body and blood of the Lord. 1 Corinthians 11:27: "Wherefore whosoever shall eat this bread unworthily shall be guilty of the blood of the Lord."

They are looked upon more like murderers than disciples. Instead of receiving benefit of His death, they contract the guilt of it in that they show a contempt of His body and blood. They no more regard His death than the Jews who crucified Him; they look on as careless spectators.

They eat and drink the body and blood of Christ rather like those who so thirsted for His blood and were ready to devour His flesh like wolves than a disciple who had a spiritual appetite for it as their proper nourishment.

In order to prepare for this ordinance:

1. Before we come to it, let us carefully and strictly examine ourselves whether we are in any way of sin, whether we neglect any duty that God has required of us, whether or not we aren't too careless in the performance of some duties, whether we haven't got in a negligent way of performing duties of religion, whether or not we aren't to little watchful over our own hearts and don't too easily give way to temptations to neglect our duty, whether we aren't too little in reading the Word of God, and whether we aren't too flighty and overtly in prayer.

We must examine ourselves whether or not we don't live in some way of commission that is provoking unto

God, or at least often fall into some sin for want of our resolving and watching against it; whether or not we don't
harbor and indulge some lust or other. If we allowedly live
in any way of wickedness and yet come to the Lord's Supper, it will dreadfully aggravate our guilt. It is most horrid
presumption in any person from time to time to come to
the Lord's Table and feed on His body and drink His
blood, and yet live in the indulgence of any carnal and
corrupt appetite, and come without any serious reflec-
tions upon themselves for it or any resolution of amendment.   Coming to the Lord's Supper thus is a horrid
profanation of the ordinance, and it does but seal their
damnation instead of sealing to them the benefits of the
gospel.   1 Corinthians 11:28: "But let a man examine himself and so eat of that bread and drink of that cup, for he
that eateth and drinketh unworthily eateth and drinketh
damnation to himself."

Let us therefore take heed to ourselves at all times before we come to the Lord's Supper to search and try ourselves and see if there be any wicked way in us. Let us think
on our ways and turn our feet into God's testimonies,
humbling ourselves for our past sins and making serious
resolutions of future amendment.

We do in this ordinance, as I have said already, set to
our seal of the covenant of grace; we do in the most solemn way possible renew our covenant and engage to be
the Lord's. But what horrid mockery will this be if we at
the same time live in some sin and intend no other than to
do so still.

We should, before every sacrament make a set business
of examining ourselves. We should not only inquire

whether we don't live in some ill way, but should call to mind all the instances we can wherein we have dishonored God and acted unbecoming the Christian temper in our behavior towards God or towards our neighbor, and should confess the same to God, and humble ourselves and resolve to watch against the like for the future.

2. Before we come to the Lord's Supper, let us take care that we may do it in charity with all our brethren. This is one end of this ordinance, as we have already observed, viz., communion with our brethren whom we partake with, and also with all Christians throughout the whole world. This is one thing expressed by this feast, which is a feast of charity, peace and love between the members of the church; and 'tis what is engaged in it.

Therefore, before we come to this ordinance, we should consider whether or not there is a breach or interruption of Christian love, charity, and peace between us and any of our brethren, and if there is any quarrel or misunderstanding. We should do what belongs to us so that there may be an entire peace and union again. We should do our utmost, if it is possible, says the apostle, to, as much as in us lies, live peaceably with all men (Romans 12:18).

We must take heed so that at any time we don't bring with us to the Lord's Table any hatred or malice against any of our neighbors, that we don't come with a bitter and envenomed spirit against any of our brethren. If we do so it will be as leaven in the feast of old. The Jews, when they kept the Passover, if they had any leaven in their houses it defiled the festival and rendered it void. But malice is like leaven in this Christian Passover. 1 Corinthians

5:7–8: "Christ our Passover is sacrificed for us. Therefore let us keep the feast not with old leaven, neither with the leaven of malice and wickedness."

If we have done any wrong any way to our neighbor in his estate or name, or have otherwise broken or shaken his charity towards us, we must take heed that we don't presume to come to this holy ordinance before we have made satisfaction or are reconciled to our brother. Matthew 5:23–24: "Therefore if thou bring thy gift to the altar, and there rememberest that thy brother hath ought against thee, leave there thy gift before the altar, and go thy way; first be reconciled to thy brother, and then come and offer thy gift."

3. We must seriously meditate on those things that are signified in this ordinance in order to our being prepared for it. We must meditate on the Lord Jesus Christ and contemplate His glory and excellency. Meditate on the gloriousness of gospel benefits and the marvelous way wherein they are procured for us and applied to us. Then labor to obtain a lively sense of the certainty and excellency of these things.

And here, to assist our meditation, it would be profitable to make use of the Word of God and other books that treat these subjects.

4. Let us endeavor to prepare by earnest prayer to God for His presence and blessing with the ordinance so that we may see Christ at His Table, may discern the Lord's body, may indeed have communion with Christ and His people there, and that we may have in every way the suitable motives and influences of His Spirit.

5. Last, we must at all times see to it that we do our

duty in this ordinance so that the church may be kept pure from scandal, if we would have the presence of Christ at His Table. If we are an impure company, if persons who are openly scandalously are allowed to sit down with us, we can't expect the presence of Christ, or that we shall receive the blessings signified in the ordinance, and with us in particular if it is through any neglect of ours that the ordinance is thus defiled and that scandalous persons are not kept away. We shall thereby ourselves become defiled in that we are partakers of their sin and that through our neglect this holy, pure, and solemn ordinance is defiled.

Let this exhort those who come to the Table of the Lord to behave afterwards in that holy and Christian manner that is answerable to the nature and design of the ordinance.

Every time we come to Christ's table it should more and more engage us to live more to God and Christ's glory, to be more careful to avoid all sin, which is so contrary to the nature of that holy food that we have partaken of. Sin does not become those who are nourished by the body and blood of the holy Lamb of God.

We should labor to our utmost to live more as those who are the children of God, and who are the people of Christ, and as those who have been with God, and have been conversing with Christ.

We should take heed that we aren't entangled in the cares and vanities of this world, that we don't set our hearts upon such things; for that does not become those who live upon the meat that does not perish. We should converse more with God in duties of His private worship, for it becomes those who have lately had a taste of His sweetness. We should be careful to walk more according to Christian rules of behavior towards men in justice, meekness, love, and forgiveness, treating our brethren as those of the same family who eat at the same table.

If we don't do thus we shall frustrate our renewal of the covenant, and our seeking our engagements to be the Lord's and to live to His glory, which are done in the sacrament.

If we hearken to these exhortations, then we shall be in the way to enjoy that communion of benefits designed in this ordinance. And if these things were more carefully attended to, how much more would the efficacy of this ordinance appear in converting souls, in building saints up in holiness, and causing religion to flourish in our churches?

2

The Sacrament of the Lord's Supper Is a Very Sacred Ordinance

"For he that eateth and drinketh unworthily, eateth and
drinketh damnation to himself, not discerning the
Lord's body." 1 Corinthians 11:29

(Preached in January 1732)

There were many woeful corruptions and disorders
that had crept into the church of Corinth that the apostle
writes to 'em about in this epistle. There were divisions
and contentions among them that the apostle tells 'em of
in chapter 1:11: "For it hath been declared to me of you,
my brethren, by them which are of the house of Chloe,
that there are contentions among you." And 3:3–4 shows
that one said he was of Paul and another said that he was
of Christ. So they were divided into parties and separated
one from another.

Another corruption and disorder among them was
that they tolerated incest, as in chapter 5. Another was
their going to law one with another, and that before the
unbelievers, as in the beginning of chapter 6. Another was

their eating things sacrificed to idols, which the apostle treats in chapters 8–10. Another was their indecent habits in their public assemblies: men came to the public worship habited, in some respects, like women, particularly their coming with long hair. Another was that there was a party among them that denied the resurrection (chapter 15). Another was their profane and disorderly manner of attending the Lord's Supper. Many of them attended in no other manner than they would a common meal, to satisfy their carnal appetites; and some of 'em drank to excess so as, in a measure, to inebriate themselves at the Lord's Table (11:20–22). Some of 'em, it seems, were in haste to get there before others so that they might eat and drink their fill before others came, lest if they stayed till all came together they should not have enough (verse 21).

And then another profanation of the Lord's Supper was that the rich ate and drank up all. And they would not let the poor partake with them, probably because they were not able to bear their part in the charge; for the charge of the sacrament then used to be very great. They used to have a sacrament every Sabbath, as in Acts 20:7. The charge was also the greater because they made use of it as a common meal and so ate and drank in great quantities to satisfy their hunger and thirst; and therefore they would not let the poor who were not able to bear charge with them have any share.

Upon these accounts it is that the apostle tells 'em in the text that he who eats and drinks unworthily eats and drinks damnation to himself, that is, he who eats and drinks in such an ignorant, careless, and profane manner as you do, eats and drinks damnation to himself.

The end of coming to the Lord's Supper is that we might eat and drink Christ's body and blood, so that thereby we might have salvation. But those, on the contrary, eat and drink damnation to themselves, not discerning the Lord's body, i.e., not distinguishing this bread and wine from common meat and drink, either not knowing or having no regard to the special relation that it has to Christ's body.

DOCTRINE: The sacrament of the Lord's Supper is a very sacred ordinance.

All God's ordinances are holy and sacred, being all attended in the name of God and being consecrated immediately by God, having the sanction of His sacred authority, being set apart by Him for holy uses so that in them we may immediately have to do with God and may worship Him and may maintain intercourse with God and Christ.

And all God's ordinances are in some respects alike holy, for they all are established and consecrated by the same divine authority, and in them we all have to do with the same holy God. And yet, notwithstanding so, one may be peculiarly and eminently sacred and solemn because we may in some of them have to do with God in a more solemn manner than in others, and God may be represented as having to do with us in a more solemn manner in some than in others.

Among all the ordinances of divine worship that God has instituted and we are commanded to attend, the sacrament of the Lord's Supper seems to be more eminently sacred and holy, and that for the following reasons:

REASON 1. Jesus Christ in this ordinance is more especially and sensibly represented as being then and there

present. Christ is represented as being present in other
ordinances. He is represented as present in public prayers,
for we call on His name and call on the Father through
Him and transact with God in His name. He is represented
as being present in the preaching of the Word, and so in
administering church censures; for the minister does what
he does in His name as His ambassador and as representing His person (2 Corinthians 2:10). But Jesus Christ is
more visibly and remarkably represented as being then
and there present in the sacrament of the Lord's Supper.
The minister in administering this sacrament represents
Christ's person, as he does in preaching the Word himself.
Christ Himself administered the first sacrament. He Himself offered the bread and wine to the disciples, signifying
that 'tis He who offers and confers gospel benefits to
Christians.

And all His ministers in all ages, in administering the
bread and wine, represent His person. When the ministers
offer the sacramental elements, it is as representing Christ
and 'tis to be looked upon as though Christ stood there
offering it to us, and therein offering us His benefits.

But besides this Christ is represented as being then and
there present more especially and remarkably in another
way, and that is as His body and blood are there sensibly
represented. Christ is represented as being there present
to our bodily eyes, and not only to our eyes, but to our
other senses: to our touch and taste. Besides our seeing
with our eyes the outward signs and tokens of His body
and blood, we do in this ordinance, as it were, handle
Christ as Thomas did, and put our fingers into the prints
of the nails and our hands into His side.

REASON 2. Christ in this ordinance is not only sensibly represented as being present among us, but as being slain among us. This renders the sensible representation of His presence a great deal more solemn than otherwise it would be. To see Jesus Christ represented to our bodily senses by divine institution is a solemn thing; but to see Him hanging upon the cross and dying and having His body broken, His blood shed, and He expiring under the weight of God's wrath is a thing a great deal more solemn. This may appear by the consideration of several particulars:

(1) Herein Christ is represented not only as present, but as present under the most affecting circumstances possible. If Christ was represented among us as teaching us divine doctrines, telling us our duty, telling us His Father's will, therein He would be represented as being among us in a very solemn manner, but how much more when He is represented as dying among us, when He is set forth as lifted up on a cross and tormented to death in our sight and all we standing round to see it, to see His blood trickle from His wounds till He dies.

When Christ was on earth, the disciples were with Christ when they saw Him with their bodily eyes, when they saw Him working miracles. That was a solemn thing when they heard Him teaching and preaching the gospel; it was a solemn thing to be there present, but it was a more solemn thing, a great deal more solemn, when they came to stand by and see Him crucified.

Christ never was in so affecting circumstances as when He was dying. He was in circumstances that were very remarkable at His birth, when He was brought forth in a stable and laid in a manger. He was in remarkable and wonderful circumstances when He was carried away into the wilderness and there suffered the temptation of the devil. He was in affecting circumstances when under those latter sufferings that He met with from time to time in the course of His life. But never was He in such affecting circumstances as when He was hanging upon the cross under the pains and agonies of death and God's wrath.

It is a solemn thing to stand by and see any person die, though it is but by sickness. It is a more solemn, affecting sight to see a person put to a violent death. How solemn a thing then must it be to see the Son of God, the Creator and Holy Lord of heaven and earth, dying and being put to a violent death, a death of inexpressible pain, torment, and agony. 'Tis spoken of in Scripture as a great thing to have Christ visibly represented as crucified before our eyes. Galatians 3:1: "Before whose eyes Jesus Christ hath been evidently set forth, crucified among you."

The crucifixion of Christ was the most solemn thing that ever came to pass in the world; and we well suppose it to be the most solemn thing that ever the eyes not only of men, but angels saw. The greatness and solemnity of it was signified by the great things that happened at that time, when the sun ceased shining and there was darkness over all the world, and the veil of the temple was rent, and the earth did quake and the rocks were rent (Matthew 27:51).

(2) Herein this ordinance is the special memorial and representation of the most eminently holy act that Christ performed while on earth. The death of Christ is to be considered not only as His passion, but as His action. Christ was not only passive, but active in laying down His

life. John 10:18: "no man taketh it from Me, but I lay it down of Myself."

He came into the world for this end, that here He might lay down His life. He offered a sacrifice in it. He made His soul an offering for sin; offering a sacrifice is an action. Consider Christ only as a sacrifice, and so offered He was passive in His death; but consider Him as the Priest offering the sacrifice, and so He was active. And Christ's offering this sacrifice to God was the most eminently holy act that Christ did while on earth.

Offering sacrifices of old, though they were but typical sacrifices, was accounted a very sacred and holy work. The sacrifices in the Old Testament were called most holy things, as in Exodus 30:10, and in many other places. In the original it is "holies of holies," and the priests were reckoned a very holy Order of men upon that account, because they were concerned in so holy a work as sacrificing. Leviticus 21:6: "They shall be holy unto their God, and not profane the name of their God, for the offerings of the Lord made by fire and the bread of their God they do offer; therefore they shall be holy." But if the sacrificing of bulls, goats, and calves was such a sacred, holy work, how much more a holy act must this be, the eternal Son of God's offering up His own body and soul in sacrifice to God?

The typical sacrifices of old were so holy that they were to be attended in a very sacred and reverent manner. Then certainly should this great and infinitely more holy sacrifice be so attended, and the memorial and representation of it that there is in the Lord's Supper?

This act of Christ in offering Himself up in sacrifice to

God was a most eminently holy action because His holy and infinite love to God the Father, and His respect for His glory, were therein above things manifested; for this He did from love for His Father and out of respect for His glory. When He had a mind to redeem man, such was His infinite regard for the glory and honor of God that He was willing to die rather than that man's redemption should be inconsistent with His glory—and His death has made it not to be inconsistent with it.

And then Christ's offering up Himself was an act of obedience to the Father, for He had received this command of the Father, that He should lay down His life. John 10:17–18: "Therefore doth My Father love Me, because I lay down My life that I might take it again. No man taketh it from Me, but I lay it down of Myself. I have power to lay it down and I have power to take it again. This commandment have I received of My Father."

This is therefore the most eminent act of Christ's mediatorial holiness or righteousness, of that obedience that is imputed to us. The Lord's Supper is a special commemoration of this most holy act of Christ, and therefore is an eminently holy ordinance.

(3) It is herein the special memorial of that greatest manifestation of the divine perfections that ever was given to the world. The work of redemption is the greatest of all the works of God, a work of which the first creation was but a type. And the death of Christ is the principal thing in the work of redemption, the most wonderful thing belonging to it; 'tis by this principally that the work of redemption is performed; 'tis by the death of Christ, the blood of Christ, that we are redeemed. This was the price that was

paid, and by which we were purchased.

The glory of God never so clearly and brightly shone forth as in this; it shines forth here to the admiration of the angels. They never saw such a manifestation before of it in any work that ever they saw done (1 Peter 1:12). The wisdom of God never was so manifested as in this, in accomplishing the redemption of man by the death of the Son of God. The justice of God never had such a manifestation as in the sufferings of Christ. And this is especially the most glorious manifestation also of the goodness and grace of God that ever was given to the world. The goodness of God appears much in God's making the sun to give us light, in giving rain, in giving blessedness to the angels. But these are nothing in any comparison with His giving His Son to die.

(4) Last, the Lord's Supper herein is a special representation and memorial of the greatest and most wonderful thing that ever came to pass. Look not upon it under any particular consideration, but look upon it in the general; and 'tis the greatest and most wonderful thing that ever came to pass of any kind whatsoever. There was never any event to be compared to it for wonders. What was there that ever came to pass in anywise wonderful like this, or what can be conceived of so wonderful as the Son of God, the eternal Jehovah, God almighty, God blessed forevermore, the Alpha and Omega, the great Creator and Lord of heaven and earth dying a cursed and ignominious and tormenting death.

There have many great and strange things come to pass in the course of God's providence at one time and at another, but never any to be compared to this. When the

Son of God became man and was born of a virgin, became an infant in a manger, that was a great and strange thing, but not so great as dying on the cross. This ordinance therefore that is instituted and attended in remembrance of this and wherein this thing is represented must be eminently sacred.

REASON 3. But we now come to the reason why herein is not only a sensible representation of Christ as slain amongst us, but as slain for us. Here is represented His being slain for our benefit. The bread is broken and the wine poured out for us; here Christ is represented as being slain to make a feast for us, He being slain so that we might feed upon Him, so that we poor souls might be kept from famishing and perishing and might have life. John 6:51: "The bread that I will give is My flesh that I will give for the life of the world." Here is represented Christ dying, shedding His blood out of love for us and His giving Himself slain unto us. The bread is broken and wine poured out, and then given to us by Him who represents the person of Christ. Here is a sensible representation of Christ's offering His body and blood to us, broken and spilt so that we might have life, so that here we don't only see Christ in the most affecting circumstances possible, as being in circumstances of extreme suffering, but as being in those circumstances for our sakes. Herein we don't only see Christ in the most holy act that He performed while on earth, but doing that act for us so that it might be our righteousness. Herein we don't only see that work of God that is the most wonderful discovery of His perfections that ever was, but we see that work wrought for ourselves. We don't only see the greatest and most wonderful thing that ever came to pass, but we see it accomplished for us out of grace and love to us poor, sinful worms of the dust. This renders the occasion more sacred, solemn, and affecting unto us. So much the more cause is there for our attending on it with great attention and regard.

REASON 4. The nearest possible concern with Christ is both represented and designed in this ordinance. Our nearest possible concern with Christ is in this ordinance sensibly represented. When we come to this ordinance and here see Christ Jesus slain amongst us and slain for us, we don't sit by as idle spectators who have nothing to do, but see it as having to do with Christ slain in the most near and intimate manner conceivable, as appears in these two particulars:

First, in this ordinance is sensibly represented our communion in the slain body and shed blood of our Redeemer. The body of Christ is first slain, His blood shed, and then 'tis given to us; and we partake of it and we receive it and eat and drink it.

This is much more than merely seeing His body broken and His blood shed. Our concern with the broken body and shed blood is much more than looking on it with our eyes comes to. But when we have seen it, then we take it, we have it, and we taste it and make use of it as our meat and drink.

They who came to the sacrifices did not stand there only as spectators to see the sacrifice slain, and some of it burnt on the altar; but when it was done they partook of it. They eat of it before the Lord; so it is with respect to the great sacrifice of the body and blood of Christ.

What more near concern can be conceived with a slain

Savior than eating and drinking of Him and having Him turned into nourishment that our natures may partake of Him and be nourished strengthened and increased by Him. Believers have an exceedingly near concern with Christ crucified. He is their spiritual food; they are united to Him in the most intimate manner. 1 Corinthians 6:17: "He that is joined to the Lord is one spirit," and they have communion with Him and with one another in Him. They do, in union with Him, partake with Him of His nature, of His Spirit, His life and His joy, His happiness; and all this by His body and blood. 'Tis by the slaying of His body and spilling of His blood that we receive those benefits as much as by meat and drink that our bodies receive strength and refreshment.

Second, in this ordinance is a representation of the most friendly and intimate conversation with Christ and enjoyment of Him. This is not only a feast wherein we feed upon Christ, but wherein we feast with Him. Christ invites us to a feast and He invites us home to His own house to sit at His table, and there to eat and drink with Him. So we are to consider Christ as represented as sitting with us, feasting with us, and we feasting with Him as His guests.

Now this represents our conversation with Christ. Sitting with Him at the same table represents our being conversant with Him as His friends and guests, and being admitted to society with Him. This also represents our enjoyment of Christ. Feasts are made for friends' enjoyment of each other, for the expression of their love and kindness one to another, and for the better advantage of the enjoyment of each other's company.

This feast is a marriage feast; it represents that spiritual

feast that in Scripture is called the marriage supper of the
Lamb (Revelation 19:9). We read in Matthew 22 of a king
who made a marriage supper for his son, and sent forth
and invited from the highways and hedges the poor. This
king is God the Father and His Son is Jesus Christ. 'Tis this
marriage feast of the Son of God that is represented in this
ordinance; and so here is represented that holy joy and
spiritual mirth that believers have in Christ. In the Lord's
Supper is a representation of the saints' enjoyment of
Christ in heaven; by the wine in this sacrament is represented this new wine that the saints drink with Christ in His
heavenly Father's kingdom. Thus Christ said when He partook of the first sacrament with His disciples. Matthew
26:29: "I will not drink henceforth of this fruit of the vine
until that day that I drink it new with you in My Father's
kingdom."

But how is that joy and blessedness that is enjoyed in
His Father's kingdom called this fruit of the vine? He can't
mean any otherwise than as that is represented by this.
Christ calls His saints' enjoyment of blessedness with Him
in glory eating and drinking at His table in His kingdom.
Luke 22:29: "And I appoint unto you a kingdom as My Fa-
ther hath appointed unto Me that ye may eat and drink at
My table in My kingdom."

Second, 'tis the special design of this ordinance to be a
means of this most near and intimate concern with Christ.
This near concern with Christ is not only sensibly represented in it, but is the end of it; 'tis the thing especially
aimed at by it. It was a special end of Christ's instituting
the ordinance that it might be a special means of our
communion in His body and blood.

The end of this eating and drinking of what represents
His body and blood is that we might really eat and drink
His body and blood spiritually so that we might be united
to Christ so that we might, by virtue of the sacrifice of His
body and blood, be partakers of His nature, His life, and
His happiness.

'Tis the end of this outward and sensible representation of our friendly conversing with Christ and enjoying
the manifestations of His love at His table. The design of it
is that this might be a means of our conversing with Christ,
indeed sitting with Him at His table and feasting on His
spiritual dainties. 'Tis aimed at in it that we should feed on
Christ and feast with and spiritually converse with Him and
rejoice in Him then in the time of it, and that we might be
led and helped to it in the course of our lives, and that we
might be fitted to drink new wine with Him and eat and
drink with Him in His Father's kingdom.

This ordinance may well be looked upon as much
more sacred by reason of this near concern with Christ in
it. So much the more nearly we are concerned with God
in any thing, so much the more sacred and solemn is it.
The more nearly we have to do with Christ upon any occasion, the more holy is that occasion.

REASON 5. This ordinance is very sacred because
herein a mutual covenanting between God and us is most
solemnly renewed and sealed. This mutual covenanting
that there is between God and His people is never more
solemnly transacted than it is in this ordinance. The covenant then is most solemnly renewed and sealed on God's
part, and renewed and sealed on our part. Those actions
that are performed by the minister in breaking the bread

and wine, and offering them as the signs of the body and blood of Christ to us, are God's solemn renewal of the covenant to us.

In the minister's offering the bread and wine, Christ renewedly offers Himself and the benefits of the gospel to us; and the language of it is a promise that if we will accept them truly and sincerely we shall have them. Christ offers us His body and blood, that is, the benefits procured by His body and blood in the gospel; but in this ordinance He solemnly renews this offer and does, as it were, say to us, "Here is My body and blood slain and spilt. I offer it to you; if you will receive it and accept it, you shall be possessed of it. I require nothing of you but your acceptance; if you accept the benefits and blessings that I have purchased, I promise that they shall be yours." Christ here renewedly offers Himself with all that He is and has to each one of us who sits at His table.

It is done in the most solemn manner. It is done in the preaching of the Word, but 'tis done in a more solemn manner in the sacrament; for here He does it and adds a visible seal to it. There are those actions and sensible signs that God has appointed representing the conferring of the blessings promised, signifying that they shall be infallibly conferred if we perform the condition. So here is a most solemn renewal of the covenant on our part.

In this ordinance we make the most solemn profession of the Christian religion, and of God as our God and Christ as our Savior, that ever is made. There is a profession of religion implied in our coming to meetings and attending the public prayers and singing God's praises, and the preaching of the Word, but not so solemn as in the

Lord's Supper.

This is the language of our accepting the bread and wine after it is broken and poured out, that will take Christ crucified as our only Savior, our Lord, and our only portion. A promise that will we be devoted to Christ and will take Christ as our Savior can't be more solemnly made than this. In taking the signs of His very body and blood, and eating and drinking them, we seal the promises that we make by this action. And how can we in any way more sincerely and solemnly seal our profession than by such an action? This is much more than merely coming to meetings and attending public prayers and preaching, though there is a profession of Christianity implied in that.

Thus I have in some instances shown how the Lord's Supper is an ordinance that is eminently sacred and holy.

Application

USE 1. If it is so, then what are we to think of those who turn their backs upon it and cast a visible contempt upon it? It is with respect to this ordinance as it is when persons are invited to a feast. If a king, out of his royal bounty and grace, should make and great feast and invite a great number of poor men to come and be his guests, if they should some of them turn their backs upon his invitation and refuse to come, would not that be an open affront, a visible contempt, cast upon the king's gracious offer and invitation?

We read in Matthew 22 of a certain king who made such an invitation to a feast. Did not they who turned their backs upon the invitation and refused to come cast a visi-

ble contempt upon the king's great bounty and condescension, that he should invite them to the wedding supper of his own son? He sent once and again, but they
would not appear. It was said that they made light of it.
And certainly this was the look and language of their turning their backs as they did, and going one to his farm and
another to his merchandise.

The Lord's Supper is a feast that God has provided for
us, and all are invited to come; all universally are called as
it is in the invitation to the spiritual gospel feast. So it is in
this outward representation of it: all are invited. We are
invited to come freely; no hard terms are exacted of us,
but we are invited to come without money and without
price. We stand in great need of coming, for our souls are
in a famished condition. And here are rich supplies for
our souls. Therefore persons going away must necessarily
be a visible dishonor and contempt of this holy ordinance.

If this ordinance is so holy and sacred as we have heard
under the doctrine, then surely there ought to be the
greatest respect shown to it. It ought to be honored by us.
What is very sacred ought to be highly esteemed and
prized by us. If we cast contempt upon that which is so
holy and sacred, God will require it of us. There is such an
eminent sacredness in this ordinance that to cast open
contempt upon it must render persons very guilty in the
sight of God.

I am aware that some persons have many excuses for
their turning their back upon this ordinance. Particularly,
some of them plead that they are not fit to come to such a
holy ordinance. But here I would inquire what they mean
by their unfitness. First, if they mean by their unfitness that

they aren't concerned about the salvation of their souls, that they have such a contempt of Christ and His benefits that they have no great desire of 'em and don't think 'em worth their seeking in all the ways of God's appointment.

I answer, this that is your condemnation is no excuse for your not coming. But if that is their unfitness, that they don't seriously desire Christ and His salvation, so as to be willing to seek Him with seriousness and diligence in all the ways of God's appointment, that is so far from excusing their contempt that it shows their contempt.

Your contempt consists in this; it is your condemnation that you are no more seriously engaged in your mind to seek Christ and His salvation and benefits, that you aren't willing to forsake all your sins to come to the sacrament. And so, if you should come, it would not be as seriously aiming therein at the spiritual and eternal benefit of your soul, and earnestly seeking it.

But if you are sensible of your need of Christ and His salvation, so as to be willing seriously and earnestly, and above all things to forsake all sin for the sake of it, and seek it in all the ways of God's appointment, you are one who is evangelically fit. 'Tis true, you are unworthy to come to the Lord's Supper, or of the least mercy in the world; but if your unworthiness is what you acknowledge and lament and deplore, you are one who is evangelically fit.

But if by your unfitness you mean that you don't live well enough, that you live in evil practices that you aren't willing to part with, then you don't look upon yourself solemnly and seriously enough to come to so holy an ordinance. You don't know how to forsake these and those customs, your ill company, and such and such lusts that are dear to you.

To this I answer, this is so far from being an excuse to you that it renders you the more exceedingly guilty and inexcusable. You are still pleading your contempt as an excuse for your contempt. It shows that the way that you live in is a way of known wickedness, that you yourself think it is such as makes you unfit to come. That shows you know it to be wicked or else you would not think it made you unfit. If it is no sin, why are you the less fit for it? And are you so ridiculously foolish as to imagine that your will-fully unfitting yourself for a duty is an excuse for your ne-glect of that duty? It is as if a master commands a servant to come into his presence, and the servant willfully strips himself naked and makes himself unfit.

That you will willfully do thus doesn't show your con-tempt of this holy and sacred ordinance to be the less, but the more. Only turning your backs upon Christ and His benefits, as you do by going away from the sacrament, shows contempt; but to turn your back to go away to your idols is to sin willfully against that Redeemer who therein shed His precious blood and invites you.

We read of going away, one to his farm and another to his merchandise: that showed that they made light of it. But these go away to their drunkenness, to their lascivi-ousness, to other practices of known wickedness, or to the service of their lusts.

Again, if you say that you are sinful, that you see so much sin and corruption in yourself, so much the more you need to come and receive Christ's body and blood.

The more terrible your distemper that you have, the

more is your famishing state, so much the more you need
to come and receive this spiritual food. The more blind
you are, so much the more you need to come to Christ,
and to this visible representation of Christ and His body
and blood.

What was the gospel feast made for but to have eyes
become sober, but for the supply of the sinful, wretched,
and miserable? And this feast that represents Christ is
made for the same end.

The poor and maimed and halt and blind were invited
to the marriage supper (Luke 14:21). They did not make
their poverty, their nakedness, their lameness, or their
blindness an excuse, but went the rather, more in need of
going.

But, again, you say you are unconverted and shall
come unworthily. And it is said that he who eats and drinks
unworthily, eats and drinks damnation to himself.

To that I answer, I would not desire you to come as the
Corinthians did of whom the apostle speaks, to come to
satisfy your carnal appetite, to get drunk, to make use of it
as a common thing, making no distinction between this
and your common food, not discerning the Lord's body,
either being ignorant of the relationship or having no regard for it. I would not desire you come in a careless and
profane manner. I don't desire you to come unless you
are concerned for the good of your soul. I don't desire
you to come directly from the practice of drunkenness or
lasciviousness, and then to go from this holy ordinance directly to it again.

I would have you to seek God and your salvation in all
the ways of His appointment, and in this among the rest.

Come in a serious manner, taking great care to examine yourself whether you are in the faith, reforming all known sin before you come. Come with a serious desire and endeavor after the good of your soul in coming, and attending on it in the most solemn and reverent manner.

USE 2. If this is an ordinance so eminently sacred and holy, then what are we to think of those who come in a profane and careless manner, taking no care to prepare for it by prayer or any consideration or examination of themselves? What are we to think of those who come without any consideration of the sacredness of the ordinance, taking no care how they behave themselves at the Lord's Table, what they are thinking about while they attend it, who in no way seriously endeavor to attend it in a devout and reverential manner? Thus did the Corinthians, whom the apostle has respect to when he says that he who eats and drinks unworthily eats and drinks damnation to himself.

USE 3. What we are to think of those who come to the Lord's Supper and yet allow themselves at the same time in ways of known sin, who come away from acts of uncleanness or injustice, or other vicious acts, who come here and attend this most sacred ordinance and sit and behold the sensible representation of Jesus Christ in such affecting circumstances, dying under extreme agonies of body and mind. These therein attend the special memorial of the most holy act of Christ, the most glorious manifestation, the greatest and most wonderful thing that ever came to pass and see this represented as being for us, and here handle and eat and drink that which is sacramentally the body and blood of Christ, and pretend to sit with Christ at

His Table, to have communion and society with Christ in the most solemn manner possible, promising to forsake all sin, to take Christ for their Lord and as a token and seal of this promise take and eat and drink the signs of His body and blood.

And yet these are but just come from their wicked acts and continue in their wicked practices; they are still in their willful disobeying and dishonoring Christ and haven't repented of it at the same time that they are looking on and seeing Christ.

Yea, at the same time that they are eating and drinking they have no other design than of still going on in the same practices, though they know 'em to be sinful. Accordingly, they rise up from the Table of the Lord and go away again straight to the same practices, and so fill up the time between sacrament and sacrament. What a horrid profanation of this most holy ordinance are these guilty of. They trample the slain body and shed blood of the eternal Son of God in the mire of their sins; they do little better, if at all, than the Jews did who crucified Christ and mocked up while He was hanging on the cross. The apostle himself is witness in the verse before our text: "Whosoever shall eat this bread and drink this cup of the Lord unworthily shall be guilty of the body and blood of the Lord." What is said in the text is also true of them, that they eat and drink damnation to themselves.

USE 4. Lastly, if the sacrament of the Lord's Supper is so sacred and holy, how much should it be prized and delighted in by us. The more holy it is, the more excellent it is, and the more is it to be esteemed and loved by us. The more sacred, the greater privilege it is to be admitted to it, and the greater occasion there is for us to rejoice in it and to attend with exceeding joy.

What joy may it well cause in us when we see sensibly represented by Christ's own appointment Christ manifesting so great a love for us, to see Christ offering Himself slain for us, Himself to be our food for the relief of our poor, perishing souls.

How should we rejoice when we attend that ordinance wherein is represented so near concern in the communion of His benefits, so friendly a conversation with Christ, an ordinance, the design of which is to bring us to the actual possession of those blessings.

How should we rejoice when we see Christ so solemnly renewing and sealing His covenant engagements to us. And how joyfully should we comply and answer His offers by renewing and sealing our engagements to Him.

3

The Lord's Supper Ought to Be Kept Up and Attended in Remembrance of Christ

Luke 22:19: "This do in remembrance of Me."
(Preached in June 1734)

These words are a command or precept of the Lord Jesus Christ concerning which we may observe who are here commanded, or whom Christ speaks to when He says this, and that is to all His followers. The words indeed are spoken more immediately to His disciples who then accompanied Him; but Christ means all Christians to the end of the world no less than them. 'Tis common that Christ, in His delivering His rules and precepts for the direction of His people, directs Himself most immediately to His disciples. So it is throughout His sermon on the mount: it is said in the beginning of Matthew 5 that He went up into a mountain, and when He was set His disciples came unto Him and He opened His mouth and taught them. So in the commands that He left: when He was about to leave the world, He says, speaking to John, His disciple, "A new commandment I give unto you, that ye love one another" (John 13:34).

But in speaking to them, He spoke to all Christians throughout all ages, delivering in like manner as God in the Ten Commandments said from Mount Sinai, "Thou shalt not do thus or thus," speaking to the congregation of Israel there present, but not meaning only them, but all His people to the end of the world.

Observe what is the action or performance that is implied in the words, "This do," that is here commanded, which is the maintaining and attending that ordinance that He had now set them an example of when it is said, "this do." It refers to what we have an account of in the words immediately preceding: "He took the bread and gave thanks and broke it and gave unto them saying, 'This is My body which is given for you. This do in remembrance of Me," i.e., "as I now have taken bread and given thanks and broken it and given it to you to eat, so do you do this after I am gone into heaven in remembrance of Me."

It may be understood as a commandment to both ministers and people. Christ, in saying to the disciples, "This do," might mean, "You do as I have now done, and give thanks. Take bread and break it and give to others as I now have done to you." And if we understand the words, so we must look upon Christ as speaking to them as ministers; for we know that the disciples were all appointed to be ministers. In saying to the disciples, "This do," He may have respect to their taking and eating this bread that He now gave them; for in so doing the disciples acted not as ministers, but as private Christians. Christ, in that case, was the minister and they the people; but the command doubtless reaches both ministers and people. 'Tis a command to the whole church to keep up these observances that Christ has now set an example of.

Observe the manner and end of performance in re-membering Him. Christ was now about to depart out of the world. He institutes this ordinance for His people to remember Him by when He is gone. While Christ was with them before His death approached, He did not appoint this ordinance because He was yet with them and they did not need such memorials to remember Him by, and also because the Jewish dispensation yet lasted and the Passover, one ordinance of that dispensation, in the room of which the Lord's Supper was instated, was not yet abolished. The Jewish dispensation was abolished by Christ's death, and the Christian dispensation began. Therefore Christ eats His last Passover and then, when He had done that, He immediately institutes the sacrament in the room of it; and also because while Christ was with them His death had not actually been, and therefore could not properly be remembered.

DOCTRINE: The Lord's Supper ought to be kept up and attended in remembrance of Christ.

PROPOSITION 1. 'Tis the duty of Christians to keep up and attend the Lord's Supper.

1. This observance ought to be kept up in the church to the end of the world. There are some, as particularly the Quakers, who deny this, who say it was an ordinance appointed only to be kept up for a little while in the primitive church till heathenism was overthrown and Christianity came to be settled in the world. But there is no such limitation in the command. The words of Christ, "This do in remembrance of Me," refer to all Christians to the end of the world. The apostle so interprets the words in 1 Cor-

inthians 11:26. The apostle, having there told how Christ instituted the Lord's Supper and commanded His followers, saying "This do in remembrance of Me," adds, "for as oft as ye eat this bread and drink this cup ye do show forth the Lord's death till He comes."

And the reason of the thing plainly shows that it should be so. Christ instituted this ordinance when He was going away so that His people might have it to remember by when He was gone. The reason of the institution was that He was going away. He appointed this rite for them to remember Him by because of His absence; and therefore the reason holds as long as His absence holds, which is till He comes again. Therefore this memorial of Christ's should be kept up in all Christian churches throughout the world, and no society of Christians can excuse themselves in omitting it.

2. As it ought to be kept up in the church, so it is the duty of particular Christians to attend it. We find such a command of Christ extant in our Bibles: "This do." This command was given to His followers, and has nothing more to restrain or limit than any other command of Christ to Christians. It does as much bring a duty upon all Christians as such commands as these: "Love thine enemy." "Love one another." "When thou prayest, enter into thy closet" (Matthew 6:6). "Abide in Me and I in you" (John 15:4). We have no more reason to suppose the command in the text to be directed only to some Christians and not to all any more than any of these; for the command is given forth in the very same manner.

This command was given forth by Christ to His followers, or to Christians; and this is the foundation of the

command as it respects them, that they were Christians, as
followers of Christ. And therefore they should observe this
memorial of Christ.

Who should keep up memorials of Christ but Christians, those who are followers of Christ? And what reason
can there be given why all those who are the followers
should not keep up memorials of their Lord and Master?
Surely they don't act like Christians who refuse to commemorate Christ. If persons profess themselves to be
Christians, they ought to act like Christians so that their
practice and profession may agree together and that they
may not act inconsistently with themselves, making a show
as though they were Christians in some things and in others as though they would have nothing to do with Christ.

PROPOSITION 2. This ought to be done in remembrance of Christ. I would speak to this proposition in answer to the following inquiries:

1. What is meant by doing it in remembrance of Christ?

2. What of Christ is to be remembered by us in our attendance on this ordinance?

QUESTION 1. What is meant by observing this ordinance in remembrance of Christ?

ANSWER 1. One thing intended is that the church
should maintain this ordinance as a means to keep up the
memory of Christ and the transactions concerning Him in
the world so that it may not be utterly forgotten that ever
there were these and those things transacted related to
Jesus Christ, or that ever there was such a person in the
world. There have been many things that have been transacted in the world that are now wholly forgotten; many
kings have reigned, many battles fought, and many great

things done that are not forgotten. There are no records or accounts of them; the memory of them has wholly perished out of the world. And so might the whole story of Jesus Christ have been utterly forgotten before this time had not God taken care to appoint means to keep up the memory of it in the world.

There are several outward means that God has appointed, that God has given to the world, with histories of these transactions, standing records. Another is His appointing an order of men to preach these things and to keep up the memory of them. Another is that appointment of the Lord's Day to be kept, being much in remembrance of the work of redemption; and another is the Lord's Supper, an observance to be kept up in the church as a memorial of Christ. These are the means that God has made use of to keep alive the memory of those things in the world. Were it not for such care that God has taken, the world would be as liable to forget the whole history of Christ as many other parts of history and, upon some accounts, more apt.

If it had not been for the care God has taken, it is probably that in these and other things by this time it would not have so much as been known that ever there was such a person as Jesus of Nazareth in the world; for there are some parts of the world that once were famous for Christianity that, notwithstanding all this care, in a great measure forgotten—hardly anything of the story of Christ is known among them. But it never shall be wholly forgotten, but these institutions will be a means of keeping up the memory of them through all ages till Christ comes the second time.

ANSWER 2. Another thing meant by doing it in remembrance of Christ is that we should do it to renew and assist our thoughts and mediations of Christ, not only to keep alive the memory of the cross of Christ in the world, but to revive the thoughts of Christ in particular persons. 'Tis fitting that Christians, those who are Christ's disciples, should often think of their Lord and Master. Christ is a Christian's life and light, his Savior and portion; yea, He is all in all. His thoughts and meditations should therefore be much on Him. And to that end God has provided means to renew the thoughts of Him, among which the sacrament of the Lord's Supper is one of the principal ones. We should attend the ordinance of the Lord's Supper to that end, to assist our meditation on Christ, to fix our minds to give us lively ideas of Christ and the things of Christ, and a more lively sense of Him.

ANSWER 3. Another thing meant by "Do this in remembrance of Me" is that we should do it to revive suitable affection towards Christ, not merely to revive thoughts of Christ in our understanding, but also suitable exercises towards Him in our hearts. Merely to have a thought of Christ in our minds without any good effect of it in our hearts is to no purpose. We had as good not think of Him as to have no good effects of these thoughts upon us. When we speak of remembering our friends that we are absent from, we don't mean only thinking of them, but having continued and renewed affections to them, still to retain respect in our hearts for them.

Thus we ought to remember Christ in the Lord's Supper, not with a cold, dull thought, but with an affectionate remembrance of Him, with love for Him, admiration of

Him, delight in Him, and desires after Him. We should do as was said of them in Acts 2:46: "And continuing daily with one accord in the temple and breaking bread from house to house did eat their meat with gladness and singleness of heart."

ANSWER 4. Another thing implied in our doing this in remembrance of Christ is the doing of it as a testimony of our respect for Christ, not only that we should do it to keep alive our respect for Christ and to revive it in our hearts, but to testify and declare it. When it is said that we should do it in remembrance of Christ, the meaning is not only that we should do it so that we might remember, but that we should do it to show our remembrance of Him, to show what a respectful, honorable remembrance we have of Him. The design of it is that we should pay respect to Christ. In order to our doing it in remembrance of Him we should do it for His glory, seeking His glory in it. The action of receiving the bread and wine is appointed as a testimony of our respect to Christ, to be a sight of our receiving and entertaining Him. We should testify our respect for Christ in this ordinance by giving up ourselves entirely unto Jesus Christ, making a solemn, renewed dedication of ourselves to Him. That is the first inquiry.

QUESTION 2. What of Christ is to be remembered by us in our observance of this ordinance?

ANSWER 1. We ought to do it especially in remembrance of His last sufferings. This is the special design of this ordinance, to be a memorial of the death and last sufferings of Christ—not but that we ought to remember all His sufferings at the Lord's Supper, for His whole life was a life of suffering. And the commemoration of His last and greatest suffering ought to bring to our mind His other sufferings that were forerunners of them. But what is principally designed is to remember His last sufferings. 1 Corinthians 11:26: "As oft as ye eat this bread and drink this cup, ye do show forth the Lord's death until He comes." When Christ says, "This do in remembrance of Me," He means, "Do this in remembrance of what I underwent for you, in remembrance of what an agony I was in in the garden, how My soul was sorrowful even unto death, how I sweat great drops of blood. When you do this, remember how I was taken and arraigned and condemned like a malefactor. When you do this, remember how I was mocked, spit upon, and buffeted. When you do this, remember how I was nailed on the cross, and there hung for hours together in extreme pain and torture; what dreadful sufferings I underwent in my soul when the Father was departed from Me, and when I endured the terrible effects of His wrath for your sakes. When you do this, remember how My blood was shed, My soul poured out unto death."

When we do thus we ought to remember these things and to be affected with them, to be affected with admiration; for it was the most wonderful thing that ever happened, that so great a Person would undergo this for those who are so unworthy. Let us be affected with love and gratitude; let us be affected with sorrow for our sins.

The design of this ordinance is especially to remember the last sufferings of Christ. Therefore the parts of this ordinance are representations of those sufferings and the circumstances thereof. The breaking of the bread represents the killing of the body of Christ, destroying the frame of His body; the pouring out the wine represents the shedding of His blood unto death.

ANSWER 2. We must do this in remembrance of the glorious perfection and excellency of Christ manifested in His death. We should do it in remembrance of Christ, that is, of the Person of Christ, and not only what He did and suffered. Remember the glorious excellencies of Christ that He showed when He dwelt here on earth. When Christ dwelt here on earth, the church beheld His glory, as the glory of the only begotten Son of God (John 1:14). She should remember that glory that then she beheld now that He is gone to heaven. The sacrament of the Lord's Supper is appointed for that end, particularly for the remembrance of those perfections as manifested in His last sufferings.

This was a glorious manifestation of the perfection and excellency of Christ; herein was manifested the holiness of Christ, for this was done in obedience to the Father, showing respect to God's glory. Herein was manifested the patience and meekness of Christ, especially the wonderful grace of Christ. We should remember His excellencies and contemplate and admire them and be greatly delighted in them.

ANSWER 3. Especially we should do it in remembrance of the wonderful love to men that His last sufferings were the fruit of. The command of Christ, "This do in remembrance of Me," imparts as much as if He had said, "Do this and remember how I loved you; remember how Great My love for you was; remember how My love was so great, so strong for you that I spared not My life. Remember the bitter agonies and dreadful sufferings I underwent out of love for you. Remember what love there was in My heart towards you when I was in the garden, all in a bloody sweat. Remember what love was in My heart when in a ring of soldiers who were mocking Me, buffeting Me, spitting on Me. Remember Me staggering under the burden of Mine own cross; remember Me hanging on the cross, bleeding, tortured, and bearing the wrath of God, dying there."

Application

USE OF INFORMATION. Why are we commanded to do this in remembrance of Christ? The wisdom of Christ and His mercy in consulting our good and adapting this ordinance to our wants and circumstances is very conspicuous. I shall give some reasons:

REASON 1. Christ is infinitely worthy to be remembered by us. So excellent a person we esteem our good Friend and worthy to be remembered. Those who have shown us a great deal of kindness and respect we allow that we ought to remember them for it. But Christ is infinitely our best Friend; there is no love and kindness like His. We receive more good by Him, ten thousand times more, than it is possible anyone should receive from an earthly friend. The death of Christ is most worthy to be remembered; it is the most wonderful, the most memorable thing that ever came to pass, and is worthy to be remembered in heaven to all eternity.

The perfections and excellencies of Christ therein manifested are infinitely worthy to be remembered by us, that glory that then appeared in Him, as the glory of the only begotten of the Father, full of grace and truth; the glory of His holiness, the glory of His meekness and patience. The love of Christ that then appeared was most worthy to be remembered; never was there any such love; no other influence can be paralleled to it. Shall not we who are these poor, sinful, miserable worms who were the objects of that dying love remember it? Shall not we who were so distinguished by the grace and condescension of Christ remember it? Shall not we who have so great benefit by that dying love, who were delivered from a hell of eternal misery to eternal glory remember it? Shall not we often know it in our memories, often think of it, meditate upon it, and revive our love and gratitude to our glorious Friend who has so loved us and who has so saved us?

REASON 2. 'Tis necessary for our good that we should often remember the Lord Jesus Christ. He is that Person on whom we absolutely depend. And 'tis necessary that we should often remember Him, for if we should forget Him and be unmindful of Him, this would tend to a separation and alienation between Christ and us. And woe to us if there is a separation subsisting between Christ and our soul. We need frequently to remember Christ to excite in us acts of faith in Him. There is no believing in Christ without remembrance of Him; and if we don't believe in Him, we have no part in Him. We have need of often remembering Christ to excite in us love for Him. Without love for Christ the soul is dead. Divine love is the life of the soul.

We need often to remember Christ to excite us to imitate Him, to imitate the example of His wonderful love so that we may love one another as He has loved us, and to imitate the example of His meekness and patience, whereby He came as a Lamb. Hebrews 12:3: "for consider Him that endured such contradictions of sinners against Himself."

REASON 3. Christ is now absent from us as to His humble Person. We should therefore frequently remember Him. We don't see Christ Himself with our bodily eyes as the disciples did. He is gone into heaven to return no more till the last day. Therefore, certainly, it becomes us to remember Him. We should gladly make use of these visible representations of Him and of His dying love for us to remember Him. We need such helps to remember Christ by, for we are very apt to forget Him. The world is ready to crowd out of our minds the remembrance of Him. We should be thankful for such helps to excite in us a fresh and lively sense of Christ and of the great things He has done and suffered for us, and of His dying love.

USE OF REPROOF. This doctrine reproves those who don't attend the sacrament, who disobey this command in the very matter of it. They not only don't do this in a right manner, they don't do it at all; they wholly absent themselves from the Table of the Lord. These are persons that yet call themselves Christians and would not be ranked among the heathen, yet it has the face of an open disrespect to the Lord Jesus Christ. If we should refuse to remember a friend in our absence from him, or to do that which was a proper testimony of our friendly remembrance of him, it would look like casting off our friendship to him. So doubtless it is in this case, besides its being a direct disobedience to as positive a command as any in the Bible.

The doctrine also reproves those who, when they do attend the Lord's Supper, don't do it in remembrance of Christ. 'Tis to be feared whether or not there are not some so horribly profane and presumptuous as to live in a daily neglect of religion and don't concern themselves about pleasing God or seeking the salvation of their own souls and live in ways of known and willful wickedness who yet come from time to time to the Lord's Supper.

These, in a pang of conviction after some awful providence or some such thing, come into the church, but since that are grown secure and careless and live in wickedness, and yet come from time to time the Lord's Table, not out of any design to remember Christ; that is not their aim. They are careless how they do it and how they act. If they do but take the bread and the wine, and eat and drink as others do, they take no care beforehand to prepare. They take no care what their thoughts are upon in the time of it, and take no care how they behave themselves afterwards. They are in a way of known sin and intend still to go on in it at the same time. These don't do this in remembrance of Christ, but rather do it to mock Him and to trample on His body and blood. They horribly abuse this sacred memorial of Christ's death and eat and drink judgment to themselves (Cf. 1 Corinthians 11:29).

REASON 4. We desire not to be forgotten by Him. If He should be unmindful of us, how miserable we would be. We desire that He should remember us from day to day and consider our misery and pity us, remember us before His Father in His daily intercessions for us before God (Hebrews 7:25). And do we expect thus to be remembered by Him and yet at the same time forget Him? Shall we expect that He should be continually remembering us with infinite mercy and pity and concern for us? We desire that He should remember us in His glory (Luke 23:42), and yet we refuse so much as to attend this appointed memorial of His dying love in remembrance of Him when we from time to time turn our backs on that memorial or attend it in such a manner as rather to cast contempt upon Him than do it in remembrance of Him.

Direction 1. Let us do it in remembrance of Him so as in remembering Him to receive and embrace Him as our Savior. He is in this ordinance offered to us. In the bread's being offered, His body is offered to us. Let us receive Him for our spiritual food and spiritual nourishment. Let us remember His glorious excellencies so as that these excellencies may draw our hearts to Him and draw forth the exercises of love for Him and delight in Him.

Remember His dying love so as to accept that love which is offered to us. Remember His death and sacrifice so as to close with it as the sacrifice for our sins. Remember Him so as to depend on Him and Him only.

Direction 2. Remember Him so as to engage to live for Him. The remembrance of His excellency will help us to follow His example. Remembering His dying love engages us to give up ourselves renewedly to His service, to seek His glory in all things, to cleave to Him, and never to forsake walking closely with Him. If we suitably remember Him, it will so affect us to endear Him to us; it will so engage our hearts that we shall be greatly influenced to seek in all things to follow Him, to serve Him, and to show forth His praises.

Direction 3. So remember Him as the more to unite our

hearts to those who are His. If we aright remember Him, it will have this effect upon us. The consideration of His great love will cause us to love all who are His and bear His image. All whom He has so loved as thus to die for, we shall love for His sake.

4

The Lord's Supper Was Instituted as a Solemn Representation and Seal of the Holy and Spiritual Union Christ's People Have with Christ and One Another

1 Corinthians 10:17: "For we being many are one body and one bread, for we are all partakers of that one bread."

(Preached January 1750/51)

The main subject of this chapter is professing Christians eating things sacrificed to idols, which the apostle endeavors to dissuade the members of the church of Corinth from by various arguments. One thing that the apostle insists upon as manifesting the great absurdity of their eating things sacrificed to idols was their partaking of the Lord's Supper, and Christians' union and communion with Christ and one with another that is professed and exhibited in that ordinance.

In the text four things may be observed:

1. Christians' union with Christ. They are spoken of as the body of Christ, for when the apostle says, "we being many are one body," he means one body of Christ, as is manifest by what he says more expressly elsewhere, particularly Romans 12:5: "For we being many are one body of Christ." And 1 Corinthians 12:20: "Now we are many members yet one body," and verse 27: "Now ye are the body of Christ, and members in particular." And the like is in many other places.

Christians' union with Christ is further represented by their being the food or the bread of Christ, sometimes His house, sometimes His apparel, sometimes His food, His wheat, His good fruits, His first fruits, His pleasant fruits, and so on.

2. These representations express the union of Christians one with another, not only the one body. This is agreeable to what the apostle says in Romans 12:5: "For we being many are one body of Christ, every one members one of another."

3. These expressions signify the high nature of this union with Christ. It is a strict union: we are His body. Ephesians 5:30: "For we are members of His body, of His flesh and of His bones." These representations also imply not only that the union is strict, but that 'tis spiritual and vital. It also represents a most strict union one with another.

4. We may observe how this union of Christians with Christ and one another is exhibited and manifested, and that is by partaking of the Lord's Supper.

DOCTRINE: The Lord's Supper was instituted as a solemn representation and seal of the holy

and spiritual union Christ's people have with
Christ and one another.

To show this I will make two propositions:

1. Christ's people are strictly united to Christ and one
to another. The first thing appertaining to this union between Christ and His people is the union of hearts. In this
Christ is first. 1 John 4:10: "He first saved us." Christ from
eternity set His love on them He loved, the church, and
the fruit of His love for the elect church was His coming
into the world to die for her. Ephesians 5:25–27: "Christ
also loved the church, and gave himself for it; that He
might sanctify and cleanse it with the washing of water by
the word, that He might present it to Himself a glorious
church, not having spot, or wrinkle, or any such thing; but
that it should be holy and without blemish."

In consequence of this, believers have their hearts
drawn to Christ. And henceforward there is a mutual
complacence. This union of hearts is the first thing.

The hearts of Christ and His people being thus united,
there is another threefold union follows from it: a relative
union, a legal union, and a vital union consisting in two
things, conformity (John 1:10) and derivation (Galatians
2:20). But it must be remembered that a union of hearts is
the foundation of all.

Second, the people of Christ are united one to another. This is a consequence of their union with Christ. He
is their Head of union, having all so near a relation to one
Head. They all are necessarily nearly related one to another, having all one Father; they consequently become
one family and are brethren one to another.

Having one spiritual Husband to whom they are law-
fully espoused, it follows that they all together constitute
one spouse of Christ, and consequently must be members
one of another, as the apostle says. Having all one Head to
which they are vitally united and from whom they all receive life and spirit, as the members of the natural body do
from the head, hence they must necessarily be most strictly
united one to another as the different members of one
body, and united to Christ, being all so united to Christ
they must inevitably love one another.

This is the natural consequence of their union of heart
to Christ. They must love those who are in Him, His members. They must love those whom He loves; they must love
those who love Him; they must love those who are related
to Him; they must love those who are conformed to Him.

The consequence of the relative union is that they are
nearly related one to another. The consequences of the
vital union are that they have Christ's Spirit given to them;
therefore they must be conformed one to another. And,
being all so strictly united to Christ, they must in many
other respects have a very close union one with another;
they must all be united as one holy society, subject to the
same Lord and to the same laws.

They all must be united in the same business, which is
to promote the great design on which Christ came into
the world; they must be united in the same interest, the
same happiness, the same inheritance, the same profession
and the same worship.

Consequently, on those things there must be a sweet
harmony among all the members as to temper, as to con-

versation. There must be a natural inclination to sweet society and mutual converse one with another.

This union of Christians one with another is most beautifully seen in several texts of Scripture, such as Ephesians 4:2, 15–16, and 1 Corinthians 12:26–27: "And whether one member suffer, all the members suffer with it; or one member be honored, all the members rejoice with it. Now ye are the body of Christ, and members in particular." Acts 4:32: "And the whole multitude of them that believed were of one heart and one soul."

One thing I would observe of the union of Christians one to another is that things are not in the same order as in union with Christ. Here, relative union is first and union of hearts follows.

PROPOSITION 2. The Lord's Supper is a solemn representation and seal.

First, it is a representation of the union of Christ and His people, a union of hearts. This may be likened to a relative union, a father among his children. It may be likened to a marriage union, since the Bridegroom here is manifesting His great love and offering Himself, and the bride is receiving Him.

Here is also represented their union one with another, for here they meet together as brethren, as children of one family, as one spouse of Christ, as all united in one Head, all having communion in the same benefits, and so all united in the same interest. They are all united in heart as partakers together in the feast of mutual friendship and love.

Second, the Lord's Supper is a seal. Here we shall examine what is intended by a seal, and then look at the nature of a seal. A seal is some sign or token exhibited by any person or persons as a solemn, explicit confirmation of the thing sealed as what they profess to be their own act. Thus it is in the sealing of covenants, testaments, deeds, and all instruments whatsoever among men one towards another.

The seal is what is applied as a solemn testimony, and so it is undoubtedly in the seals of the covenant between Christ and His people. His seal confirms it as His own free act; it confirms the free compliance of His heart. And His people, with their act, give testimony of the free compliance of their hearts.

Second, we shall show how the sacrament of the Lord's Supper is a seal. And here I would observe that 'tis a seal on both parts. 'Tis a seal on Christ's part. The minister acts in that ordinance as Christ's representative. The minister's action in breaking the bread and pouring out the wine represents the offering of Christ for us; these are appointed as an open declaration and confirmation of the act of His heart. They show that He fully and freely consents to and complies with His part of the covenant. The union of His heart to His people exhibits His dying love, and His readiness to receive them into that near relation, into a vital union.

'Tis also a seal on His people, a solemn declaration and open testimony and confirmation that they make this part of the covenant, that they comply with the condition required of them, that as Christ offers, they accept. Their taking the bread and wine is a declaration that they accept Christ, that they accept that sacrifice. Their eating and drinking declares that they accept Christ as their food.

Here they openly profess their union of heart, their faith and love.

'Tis the most solemn confirmation that can be conceived of, that so far as they know their hearts they make this union their own free act and deed. It is more solemn than a mere oath. 'Tis just in this ordinance as it is in the mutual tokens of consent and acceptance in marriage. So in this ordinance the people of Christ solemnly confirm this union, and Christian love one to another. Feasts among all nations and from the beginning of the world have been used as seals of peace and friendship, such as between Isaac and Abimelech and Jacob and Laban.

Application

1. Hence such as know that they have no such union with Christ and His people ought not to come to this ordinance. How great and palpable is the absurdity. It appears by the text that the very nature and design of the ordinance is to a solemn profession and most explicit confirmation. Will any be so absurd as to say that God has appointed a holy ordinance of His worship for His honor and glory that on purpose that men might openly and on deliberation and design and most expressly and with the greatest solemnity perjure themselves after this manner?

The very language of the actions of communicants in the Lord's Supper is most plainly and evidently a testimony of acceptance, making that acceptance an open act. Outward eating and drinking of the body and blood is a sign and profession of something; and what can it be but of the thing signified? The thing signified is a spiritual eating and drinking—but that is by faith only.

'Tis with significant signs as it is with words: words are a profession of the thing signified by those words; so significant actions are a profession of the thing signified by those actions. They who know that they are not cordially united to Christ have no Christian union with the people of Christ. The very notion of a church sitting down together at the Lord's Table is God's family sitting down at this table as His children. Therefore, the design is not to make men children of God. They aren't admitted into the family so that they may be received into the family.

The very design of the ordinance is a feast of Christian love and friendship. And what friendship is it? 'Tis not a civil friendship. There are other covenants and other friendships; but 'tis a Christian friendship, a spiritual friendship, a holy Friendship. 'Tis friendship with Christ and one with another. But how can they come and seal such friendship who are no friends? How can they seal peace who have never made their peace?

The manner of a seal all the world over is an open declaring and confirming a thing to be one's free act and deed. Is it reasonable to suppose that God has appointed seals of His covenant as a testimony of a free act?

What can be meant by representing His body and blood as a sacrifice in this ordinance, and then our taking, but that we accept this sacrifice as our sacrifice to atone for our sin? And moreover I would observe that sacraments are covenant privileges and benefits. And was there ever any such thing known in any nation as a man's having a right to the benefits of any covenant or benefit but only by virtue of fulfilling the conditions of it?

2. Hence we learn the excellent wisdom in this ordinance, how suitable it is to the nature of the Christian dispensation. We see how much it tends to enliven the graces of the true people of Christ. It serves to enliven love to Christ, to cherish and love one another, and to confirm the holy friendship.

3. Hence the reason why malice does so unfit persons for this ordinance. 1 Corinthians 5:8: "Therefore let us keep the feast, not with old leaven, neither with the leaven of malice and wickedness; but with the unleavened bread of sincerity and truth."

4. Let this exhort all to endeavor to attend the approaching administration of the Lord's Supper in an agreeable manner. Let the approaching feast be indeed to us a feast of love. To this end, let us examine ourselves as to our walk. Let us cast away everything contrary to this holy union of heart. Let us examine our hearts and suppress every principal contrary, and cry to God to mortify and to inflame our hearts more and more. So this ordinance will be a resemblance of the glory of the eternal feast, and our sacraments thus attended will be sure tokens that we shall hereafter drink new wine with Christ in His Heavenly Father's kingdom.

5

The Sacrament of the Lord Is the Communion of the Body and Blood of Christ

"The cup of blessing which we bless, is it not the communion of the blood of Christ?" 1 Corinthians 10:16

(Preached August 1745)

I would speak from these words by explaining what is here affected and by applying it.

I would explain in what manner the sacrament of the Lord's Supper is the communion of the body and blood of Christ. In order to do this I would first show what is meant by communion of the body and blood of Christ. This may be done by showing what is meant by the communion and what is meant by communion of the body and blood of Christ.

1. What is meant by "communion." Partaking or enjoying any good in communion comes from the Latin *communio*. The Greek word *koinonia*, translated sometimes "communion" and sometimes "fellowship," signifies the same thing. Thus the word signifies in 1 John 1:3: "That you also might have fellowship with us." Philippians 1:5:

"for your fellowship in the gospel." Philippians 3:10 and 1 Corinthians 1:9: "who hath called us unto the fellowship of His Son." Philippians 2:1: "If any fellowship of the Spirit." 2 Corinthians 13:14: "The communion of the Holy Ghost." That is as it is expressed in 1 Corinthians 12:13: "All drink into one Spirit."

2. What is meant by the communion of the body and blood of Christ. By the word "communion" is meant a feast or a common partaking and enjoying. Now the question is how the saints are said to have this feast, partaking of the body and blood of Christ.

Here are two things to be considered: what they partake of and who they partake with. As to the former, what they partake of, it is expressed in the text: the body and blood of Christ—not that Christians do in a literal sense partake of, but these two things are intended.

It remains to be inquired who they partake with: Christians. In partaking of the body and blood of Christ they partake with Christians.

1. Having shown what is meant by Christian communion, I come now in the second place to show how and in what sense the sacrament of the Lord's Supper is the communion. It is in two respects: as it is a representation of it, and as it is a memorial of it.

First, in this holy ordinance, there is a sensible representation of this communion, a joint partaking of the body and blood of Christ. And all these great things that appertain to it, divine things, are by God exhibited, by divine appointment to mankind by signs.

There are two sorts of signs that God has instituted to signify: words and sensible representations or symbols.

Words are signs. They point forth things only as established signs. But these are not the only signs, but God Has appointed signs to be perceived also by our other senses. In sensible signs, biblical representations, is the sacrament under the Old Testament. There were a great multitude of such agreeable to the nature of that dispensation, but only baptism and the Lord's Supper remain. The sacraments are a kind of visible word.

In the Lord's Supper is the most lively and manifold representation. Here is a representation of almost everything that belongs to the first communion, as particularly:

(1) Here the person of Christ is represented by him who administers the bread and wine.

(2) The body and blood of Christ are here represented.

(3) The suffering of Christ by which way is made for the saints is in the communion represented.

(4) Christ's freely offering and giving His body and blood to the saints is here represented. Christ not only offers up His body and blood to God, He offers and bestows the benefits represented in the action of the minister, his words and actions.

(5) Believers receiving and accepting and feeding on the body and blood of Christ are here represented, both Christ's offering and believers' acting.

True believers hence see communion as a joint participation by receiving Christ's sacrifice by faith. By faith the soul accepts, as it were, it reaches out the hand and takes Christ as its food. It feeds upon Christ, i.e., receives Him as its refreshment, as its sweet, satisfying enjoyment, as its nourishment, as its strength and comfort.

(6) This is represented in their being actually the subjects of the benefits of His body and blood represented in or by the nature of the elements and their application to the receivers. The nature of the elements represents the kinds of benefits. Nourishment brings strength; bread strengthens; refreshment gives joy; wine makes glad. Psalm 104:15: "And wine that maketh glad the heart of man, and oil to make his face to shine, and bread which strengtheneth man's heart." In one word, "life." We have life by our meat and drink. Life is the summary comprehension of the benefits. Here is represented believers' union with Christ by which they have communion; here is represented for us circumstances of happiness, entertainment, and joy in that the Lord's Supper represents a feast. It represents the present happiness, as it were, a feast; it represents future happiness in heaven. Here is some representation of the blessed society above. That happiness is compared to a feast.

The good that the saints receive on earth is often represented as a feast. So the happiness of heaven is represented. Luke 14:15: "Blessed are they that shall eat bread in the kingdom of God." Luke 22:30: "That ye may eat and drink at My table in My kingdom." That the sacrifice of the Lord's Supper is a representation of this is by Christ's own words from Matthew 26:29: "Until I drink it new with you." In that particular church, that partaking together at the Lord's Supper is a representation of the church universal, with whom the saints do partake of these benefits. That little flock or company to whom Christ ministered was a representative; so is every particular company or church of Christians. In the bread's being broken for them is represented in Christ's dying for His church, as is the wine being poured out for them.

And particularly here is represented the blessed society above. As the house of God is the gate of heaven, and as the Lord's Supper is a type of that glorious feast above, so the company of saints represents the blessed society of Christians in heaven at the feast.

(7) Here is represented that union the saints have with Christ and one another by which they have communion or a joint participation. This legal union in Christ stands as their surety and their receiving vital union, union of hearts, of love in the truth of it. Their love is in attending the appointed memorial in token of gratitude, their feeding on Him, their praising Him, their union with the saints, being together as one company, as one family, one body. Love one to another, feasting together, is a token of friendship.

(8) Here is represented their joint participation itself with Christ; they partake with him who ministers in His name with the saints. Thus is the representation of all things appertaining to the saints' communion, and so is called the communion.

2. 'Tis the communion, and as it is a means of it, it means three things:

(1) By being and lively representation. It carries divine instruction as well as the Word of God. It brings to mind, keeps up the memory, fixes the contemplations, and tends to affect the heart. It leads to a sense of the wonderfulness, of the desirableness of the benefits by thus instructing the mind and affecting the heart. The sacrament is a means to all this.

(2) As a seal of this covenant, of which this communion is the great promise. A seal is an appointed sign by which any person confirms and establishes some act of his concerning some other person. So the word is used in Scripture. The Lord's Supper is a seal of the covenant of grace, a seal both on Christ's part and on ours. 'Tis a covenant wherein we are mutually concurring; both are active in covenanting. There are promises on both sides. Both therefore seal and confirm the covenant.

This is a seal on Christ's part. There are many seals of confirmation that Christ gives of His covenant. There are five kinds: His sufferings, His miracles, dispensations in the course of His providence, His Spirit, and His instruction. These last are two: baptism and the Lord's Supper. Of those aforementioned seals, the greatest is Christ's suffering, or His shedding His blood. Christ sealing the covenant with His blood is the greatest seal that ever was. 'Tis the blood or death that confirms a testament. In the sacrament of the Lord's Supper is an appointed representation of this great seal called the New Testament in His blood. Christ by His death confirmed His testimony and His promises. So all these are sealed in this representation of His death.

There is also a seal on our part. The acts of the partaker signify a receiving and giving up. The word "sacrament" originally signified an oath.

Feasts were used of old as confirmations or seals of covenants, whether covenants with God, such as Noah and Abraham, or covenants between men, such as Isaac and Abimelech (Genesis 26:28ff.), or Jacob and Laban (Genesis 31:44–46).

Covenants of God of old were sealed by sacrifices. Examples are Noah in Genesis 8, Abraham in Genesis 15, and the children of Israel in Exodus 24. Psalm 50:5: "made a covenant with me by sacrifice."

(3) A means by God's special blessing. God blesses His own institutions. Exodus 20:24: "An altar of earth," wisdom's gates, and the posts of her door.

Christ, by being with His disciples at the first sacrament, did virtually promise His blessing. And His blessing the bread and wine in the first sacrament extended that blessing. So this is a means, as 'tis God's appointed way wherein it is His revealed will that He will bestow this benefit (1 Corinthians 10:16).

Application

USE OF INFORMATION

1. The things that have been observed may give us occasion to observe the wisdom of God in the institution of His holy ordinance. It was fitting that there should be some extraordinary memorial appointed of that great event, the death of Christ, that should be constantly kept up in His church.

The wisdom of all civilized nations has led 'em to appoint memorials. It has been a thing general among the nations of the world to appoint some extraordinary memorials of very signal and remarkable events, either by erecting monuments, days to be kept in memory, or appointed certain public representation. The wisdom of nations has led 'em thus to commemorate great actions of their heroes who have been much for the public benefit,

or those things that they esteemed as remarkable favors of
their gods. But if ever any event was more worthy to be
commemorated, it is the death and last passion of Christ,
the greatest, most wonderful, most marvelous display the
divine perfections considered, with the design and events
of it infinitely greater than any of those events and heroic
acts that were so much celebrated most nearly concerns
us infinitely most for our benefit. The nations of the earth
are often wont to erect monuments in memory of great
battles and victories. But this, dear friends, when they
leave one another long and are absent, are wont oftentimes to keep some memorial of each other. But Christ is
the greatest Friend of His church, and that which is commemorated in the Lord's Supper is the greatest manifestation of His love, the greatest act of kindness that ever was
in any instance, infinitely exceeding all acts of kindness
done by man one to another. It was the greatest display of
divine goodness and grace that ever was.

Here are in this event all those things exhibited that
should be the chief subjects of our contemplation, the
chief manifestation of those things to contemplate that we
had a faculty that will be the chief subjects of the contemplation of all true Christians to all eternity. The nations of
the world are especially wont to honor their kings by keeping up memorials of things appertaining to them.

How fitting therefore was it that a memorial should be
appointed. So that the wisdom of God appears in that He
has appointed one; and not only does God's wisdom appear in appointing an ordinance that shall be a constant
memorial, but in appointing such a memorial as this
wherein the signs made use of are so simple and plain, and

yet so aptly represent the things signified. If the signs of Christ's crucifixion that were appointed to commemorate His death had been imagined—such as are used in the church of Rome—that would have been very disagreeable to the nature of true religion or would have naturally led men to idolatry; it would have that natural inclination that is in men to idolatry. If the actions had been such as were attended with a great deal of pomp and ceremony, this would have been disagreeable to the simplicity and spirituality of Christian worship; it would have drawn off our minds from the things signified to the pomp and splendor of the signs. The wisdom of God appears in appointing such a memorial not only as is a sensible figure and representation of Christ's Person and sufferings, but also so lively represents His benefits, that spiritual nourishment. In the bread is represented the most strengthening and nourishing kind of food. The chief stay of life, that spirit of refreshment, is represented by the wine. Such a representation of our communion in these benefits with so apt a representation of the grace of Christ in offering them, and of our receiving the manner in which this spiritual food is prepared for us, that is, by Christ's being Himself so apt a representation of the sweet union with Christ: Christ's love, our love, and union one with another is a representation of the heavenly society.

The wisdom of God appears in appointing such a seal of the covenant of grace to be kept up. Such a seal on His part, such actions appointed to be performed in His name as an appointed confirmation, tends to help the weakness of our faith.

Such a seal on our part, so solemn as this seal, attended with an affecting representation of those things that are the greatest motives to faithfulness by which Christ has sent us as the conceivable obligation.

This is a spiritual memorial to put us in mind of our covenant obligations that we are so apt to forget, and to engage us to carefulness that we don't forget in the midst of so many temptations to unfaithfulness. And if the nature of this holy ordinance is thoroughly considered, it will appear to be every way wisely ordered as an excellent means to promote strictness and holiness of life, and would undoubtedly prove so if it was attended seriously and carefully and with proper consideration of the nature and design of it; for here we have a sensible, affecting representation of those things that are the greatest motives to, invisible representations of, and the greatest encouragements to, God's infinite mercies.

Here are those things represented wherein consists the pleasantness and happiness of a Christian life, the glorious rewards of a Christian life and unspeakable benefits to be attained on that way. Here the engagements of Christians too are pressed solemnly and in the most affecting manner sealed and confirmed. Taking the body and blood are excellent means to engage all kinds of daily duties to God and Christ, duties of the first table of the law, duties we owe to our brethren, the sum of which is love to them. The wisdom of God in providing this ordinance appears in that herein He has dealt with us according to our nature in our present infirmed state here in the body, wherein we are affected with sensible representations and need to have things visibly represented to us.

2. The consideration of those things that here have been observed of this ordinance may make us sensible how sweet and delightful an ordinance it must be to Christians when attended as it ought to be. Herein is a lively and affecting representation of all those things wherein Christians have their great delight and happiness. Herein are represented those things that are the chief manifestations of the glory of God. His glorious perfection is represented to the church beloved. He is her dearest Friend, Spirit, and Bridegroom.

This represents those things in Him on the account of which He is amiable and sweet, those things wherein His bounty consists, of those things that were the highest manifestations of His love to the saints.

This is a representation of those things wherein their happiness chiefly consists in this world and in that which is to come. It is a representation of those duties and spiritual acts that are most sweet, and of those enjoyments. It is not only a lively representation of the most wonderful fruits of the love of Christ, but here His love is sealed. It is appointed for that end, to confirm His love, to confirm His promise and their title to it. How sweet must this render it to the saints.

Yea, the ordinance is appointed as a standing token of the love of Christ to His church through all ages. Here is a sweet feast represented, even the spiritual feast that the soul of a Christian first enjoys. Here is not only represented, but given, sweet union and communion. Both are represented and granted in this ordinance, as much as when one friend invites another to a feast at his house, and as much as when a king, to show special favor to a subject, invites him to eat with him and his family at his table.

How great is the wickedness of such as live in the careless neglect of this ordinance.

3. From what has been observed of the nature of this Holy ordinance we may learn some of the reasons why Christ has enjoined on His churches such care to remove scandals from among them.

Christ has appointed a discipline to be kept up in His church in the exercise of which churches might be kept pure from scandal, so that scandalous persons might not be tolerated among them. One end of discipline is that such persons might not sit down with others at this holy ordinance that has been spoken of; and the consideration of what has been observed of the nature of this ordinance may show us why it is very requisite that such persons as are visibly scandalous should not be admitted.

One end of this ordinance has been observed, this representation and manifestation of our union with Christ, love for Him, gratitude for our receiving Him, and giving up ourselves to Him. But while persons are openly scandalous, this is a hindrance in the way of these things.

But if persons are apparently scandalous, this hinders this visibility. Apparently scandalous persons who remain so, without visible repentance at least, if they appear obstinate, are not visible Christians. Here is something that hinders their being looked upon. Visibly wicked men must be so in the eye, and therefore can't visibly do those things that the action of Christians in the Lord's Supper are a manifestation of. This renders them no manifestation, and so they are only a mockery. There is no visible honor to Christ, but open dishonor.

And if scandalous sinners hadn't yet so persisted as to prove them so entirely obstinate, and so as visibly to destroy the visibility, yet while they remain under scandal without visible repentance, have, as it were, a suspension of the visibility of their Christianity. Till repentance is manifested, they are a stumbling block in the way of charity, a just stay to charity. And therefore, before they can be received into the company of visible saints in these solemn manifestations of their union—such as love, gratitude, and dedication of themselves—this mockery, and the scandal that caused it, should be renounced.

Again, this ordinance, as has been observed, is appointed to a manifestation of Christians' communion with Christ.

4. From what has been observed of the nature of this ordinance, we may learn why it is enjoined on Christians to examine themselves before they come to the holy ordinance of the Lord's Supper. We have this injunction in 1 Corinthians 11:28. What this examination that is required is may be learned from the type, viz., the scrutiny the children of Israel were required to make before the Passover touching all their dwellings, as may be gathered from Exodus 12:19 and 13:7.

So we are required to examine ourselves and search our hearts to see that no spiritual leaven is tolerated, if we are not living in any way of sin, if no lust is indulged. The reason why there should be such a search beforehand may appear from what has been said. If we consider that there is a manifestation and representation of a near approach to Christ, of this most intimate union and communion with Him, now surely to fit us for this we should put away all abominations. If a person was invited to feast with a king at his table, surely he would put away all that was offensive to that king.

And consider that here we profess to receive Christ, to give up ourselves to Him, and to do such in the most solemn manner, to seal our covenant with Him and to confirm our promise to Him. Now surely this should be done with care, and can't be done acceptably if we don't consider what we do, whether at this same time that we thus solemnly engage we are not living in same way contrary to such engagements. Here is that which is equivalent to the most solemn oath imaginable. But certainly such oaths should be taken without considering what we do.

Let this duty therefore and the importance of it be kept in mind and let it not be neglected.

5. From what has been observed we may learn the reason why it is especially required of Christians that they should be careful to put away all malice and ill will out of our hearts before attending. This is enjoined in 1 Corinthians 5:8: "Therefore let us keep the feast, not with old leaven, neither with the leaven of malice and wickedness; but with the unleavened bread of sincerity and truth." The apostle in the context has respect to the sacrament of the Lord's Supper. By "leaven" is signified these things: scandal, wickedness in general, and especially malice. It fitly represents scandal by reason of the infecting nature of scandal: "a little leaven leaveneth the whole lump." It fitly represents wickedness in general by reason of its sourness.

It especially represents malice because of its sourness and fermentation.

God with the greatest strictness required that leaven should be put away from the Passover. No leaven was seen in their houses and in all their quarters or they were cut off from among His people (Exodus 12:19). This is typical, and we may learn by it that it is of great importance that malice should be put away from the Lord's Supper. The reason of it may appear from those things that have been observed, that this is a memorial of the love of Christ to us who deserved His hatred, that though we were His enemies we received the most wonderful instance of love to ourselves as we hope, and on which we depend.

Now how very unsuitable is represented by our accepting these fruits of the love of Christ; our gratitude will be but mockery. Here is represented our union with the Prince of Peace and love; but what union can there be if here we seal our engagements to cleave to Him and follow wickedness; if here we profess to be His disciples, seal our engagements to cleave to Him, and go on in sin?

Here we come together as brethren, all of one family, yea, one heavenly family, children of the same heavenly Father, all children at the table of that heavenly Father who is love itself. But how disagreeable to this will it be if we bring the leaven of wickedness?

Here we appear all as one body; we are all one body and one bread. 1 Corinthians 10:17: "For we being many are one bread." But how disagreeable will such disunion be?

This is a feast of love. Here is a signification and visible expression made of our brotherly love, our union and communion, a seal of mutual friendship. Feasting together of old was used as a seal of mutual friendship. Think of Isaac and Abimelech, Jacob and Laban, and so perhaps it is among all nations. And the Lord's Supper is such a seal.

The primitive Christians had love feasts. This is especially such a feast; it is so above all others in the world, being a type of that eternal feast of the saints in heaven. It would be very disagreeable to come with malice against any of mankind, but especially any of our brethren.

Therefore let this be remembered. From time to time strictly examine yourselves as to this. Let no one come with old grudges, old sores, or secret prejudices. Doubtless, dreadful is the guilt that is often contracted because of this.

6. Hence learn with what great strictness, watchfulness, and diligence persons ought to behave themselves after an attendance on this holy ordinance. By reason of the great obligations that are laid upon us by those things that are there exhibited evidently set forth crucified, and by reason of the solemn acts we there perform, the seal we set, the vows we there renew, and the oath we swear especially shows our obligation to these two things: purity and peace. Let me therefore earnestly warn all who have this day attended that holy ordinance of the Lord's Supper and partook of the sacred symbols to remember what they signify.

7. We may learn the reason why the apostle says that they who partake unworthily are guilty of the body and blood of the Lord. This the apostle asserts in 1 Corinthians 11:27; that is, they are partakers of the guilt of murdering Him. What the apostle means by partaking unworthily may be learned from what has been said already: without care,

without previous examination, ignorantly inconsiderate, not in a serious solemn manner, without putting away leaven, without care and diligence to behave suitably afterwards. Such, the apostle says, are guilty of the body and blood of the Lord, or do, as it were, murder Christ. There are two ways of attending and beholding the crucifixion of Christ: as disciples (as those women), and as the Jews, His murderers. Both attended the crucifixion in very different ways.

So it is in the Lord's Supper: those who in this manner that has been spoken attend unworthily show contempt. They mutually consent, as if a number of them were present at the killing or murdering of a person. Suppose a great prince were murdered, while some actually stand by showing consent by laughing. All would justly be looked upon as murderers.

There are two ways of eating and drinking: one as friends and disciples, the other as blood thirsty as cannibals, says Job 31:31: "Oh, that we had of his flesh; we cannot be satisfied."

8. Hence we may learn the reason why unworthy partaking so much exposes to God's judgments. The apostle teaches that unworthy partaking brings damnation in 1 Corinthians 11:29. We may learn from what has been said that there are three sins in such an unworthy partaking that eminently expose to judgments: murder, sacrilege, and perjury. And those who are guilty of these eat and drink damnation to themselves, that is, they seal their own damnation.

There are two things that are sealed in attending this ordinance. One is by worthily partaking, the other by unworthy partaking.

Let these things, therefore, make this church to take the utmost care this day if we would not be damned, and take the most direct course to precipitate ourselves into the Lake of Fire and Brimstone.

6

Persons Ought to Examine Themselves of Their Fitness Before They Presume to Partake of the Lord's Supper Lest, by their Unworthy Partaking, They Eat and Drink Damnation to Themselves

"But let a man examine himself, and so let him eat of that bread and drink of that cup; for he that eateth and drinketh unworthily eateth and drinketh damnation to himself, not discerning the Lord's body."   1 Corinthians 11:28–29

(Preached October 1756)

The apostle in the context is reproving the disorders the Corinthians were guilty of in their public assemblies (verse 17). He first informs them that there were contentions and divisions among them and that they brought their schismatic spirit into their public assemblies with them, and manifested in their behavior. Particularly, he reproves them for their unbecoming, unworthy attendance on the Lord's Supper. They partook after such a manner as make void the ordinance (verses 20–21). They did not come to the ordinance in a religious manner and for the commemoration of Christ's death so much as to satisfy their appetites and to make use of the bread and wine of this ordinance for the same purposes as they ate and drank in their own houses.

They were wont to have the sacrament of the Lord's Supper in the primitive church very often, by all accounts of ecclesiastical history; and it seems by the account of holy Scripture that they were at first wont to celebrate this ordinance daily, as Acts 2:46: "And they, continuing daily with one accord in the temple, and in breaking bread from house to house, and afterwards weekly every Sabbath day." Acts 20:7: "And upon the first day of the week, when the disciples came together to break bread." And it coming so frequently the Corinthians, it seems, were wont to improve it for a profane use, that is, for the same end as they did their meals in their own houses, to satisfy their hunger and thirst and to nourish their bodies. And therefore the apostle says in verse 22, "What, have ye not houses to eat and to drink in?" In other words, your own houses, and not the house of God is the place where you ought to eat and drink for bodily refreshment and nourishment.

And then, it seems, they did not merely profane this ordinance by making use of the elements of it as ordinary meat and drink, but they profaned it by intemperance, especially in drinking, as the apostle intimates in verse 21. They did not profane it by gluttony, or in being intemperate in eating that bread—for there is scarcely any room for a temptation to be gluttonous in eating bread—simply they were excessive in their drinking wine.

Another abuse the apostle hints at is that they would not suffer any to partake who were poor and were not able to help bear the charge of the sacrament; or at least they contrived the matter so that they sent home them who were poor and had no houses of their own to eat and drink in ashamed and disappointed, being denied the privilege of other Christians. Everyone came to take his own supper, that which he had been at the cost of providing, so that one was hungry; that is, the poor were sent away without anything. And another was drunken; that is, those who were rich made the provision by drinking all that was provided.

So they did not attend this ordinance in that solemn manner and as seriously aiming at those purposes that were the design of the institution, doing it in remembrance of Christ's death so that they did not eat the bread with a respect to it as representing Christ's body, or drink the cup as representing His blood, but as common food. And that seems to be what the apostle means in verse 29 of their not discerning the Lord's body—that is, they did not distinguish the bread and wine from common meat and drink from the relation that they had to Christ's body and blood as representing them.

He therefore puts them in mind of the institution and the end of it, which Christ expressed (verses 23–26), and tells them how dreadfully they make themselves guilty to condemnation by showing such contempt of those sacred things that represented Christ's body and blood. And the bruising that body underwent and shedding that blood by His death, they did, by their interpretation, show a contempt of Christ Himself like that which those showed who killed Him. And by no more regarding the death of Christ exhibited in so solemn a manner in these sensible signs, they showed an unaffectedness at His death itself, and thereby a kind of consent to the act of the murderers.

In our text we have, first, the apostle's direction how to avoid eating and drinking unworthily; second, the enforcement of it. Unworthiness means unfitly, as it is often used (Revelation 3:4). Matthew 10:37: "He that loveth father or mother more than Me is not fit to be My disciple." Luke 20:35: "They which shall be accounted worthy. . . ."

DOCTRINE: Persons ought to examine themselves of their fitness before they presume to partake of the Lord's Supper lest, by their unworthy partaking, they eat and drink damnation to themselves.

In opening the doctrine we will examine:

1. What is that fitness or unfitness here spoken of.

2. What things he ought particularly to examine himself about as rendering him in this sense unfit.

3. How it behooves him thus to examine himself because, if he comes with such an unfitness, he will eat and drink judgment to himself.

1. The fitness or unfitness here spoken of is not that of desert or undeserving; there is no man upon earth who deserves such a blessing and privilege. If God had dealt with us according to our deservings, He never would have appointed us any means of grace at all. He never would have appointed such a signification and seal of His infinite mercy and grace. There are in this ordinance the exhibitions of the dying love of Christ and the offer made of the

benefits of it. Now we are all far from being worthy of such an offer. As we are unworthy of these gospel blessings themselves, so we are unworthy of the means, the signs, and the offers of them. As we are unworthy of real communion with God, so we are unworthy of such a visible signification of it.

They are not those to whom this ordinance is due that are invited to these, or those who have purchased such a blessing with money. They aren't the rich and the worthy, but the poor, the maimed, the halt, the blind, the naked, the filthy, the miserable, and the undone.

Not every unfitness renders the attendance a defective and sinful act in that manner. A man's having so much sin in his heart that he can do no other than attend the Lord's Supper in a very defective manner is not the unfitness we speak of. In this sense all men are also unworthy of any gospel privilege and are unfit for attendance on any gospel duty. If a man's being so sinful that he can expect no other if he partakes of the Lord's Supper to partake with very great and sinful defects, viz., what would be sufficient to render his partaking and eating and drinking judgment to themselves, all would eat and drink judgment.

All may confess that in this respect they are unworthy of any attendance on the Lord's Supper, and, when they have partaken, that they have partaken in a very unworthy manner. In the sense that this makes us unfit to partake of the Lord's Supper, so it renders us unfit to pray, or to come into His presence in any duty of worship.

Indeed, men offend God and might justly be condemned by Him for all sinful defects in attendance on this duty, and so they might justly be condemned for the sinful defects of their prayers.

But 'tis such an unfitness as renders the ordinance void. A man may be evangelically fit for the ordinance and yet be very unworthy of such an approach to God. He may be qualified so as to have a right to come by the gospel, and so as to have ground of encouragement of benefit in coming from God's Word, and yet attend the ordinance in a very defective manner.

But then there are some qualifications that make a man so unfit that there is no encouragement in the Word of God of any benefit to such an attendant; it is utterly against the mind and will of God that such should come bringing these unfitnesses with them. They are not designed nor appointed for such, and that for the reason because they aren't fit for it; they are not evangelically qualified.

2. Therefore, before a man comes to this ordinance, he ought to examine himself with respect to these things:

(1) Whether or not he lives in any known sin. Those persons who live immoral lives, whatever immorality it is that is their practice, who live in the customary indulgence of any lust whatsoever, are utterly unfit to come to the holy ordinance of the Lord. Whether the sin that he lives in is of commission or omission, if it is allowed and known, if he comes he comes unworthily; it makes him unfit.

Whether the sin that he lives in is lesser or greater, yet if he sins against the habitual light of his conscience, if he comes to the Lord's Table before he forsakes it, he is an unfit and unworthy partaker; and such persons had a thousand times better stay away than come. For such persons to come to the Lord's Supper is an abominable profanation of the ordinance; it is a defiling of the temple of God. Persons ought to examine whether they don't live in some former sin, some injury to their neighbor.

As of old those who were legally unclean were not allowed to come to the Passover or to eat of the sacrifices, so neither are men who live in wicked practices of any kind allowed to come near to the holy ordinance of the Lord's Supper. God doubtless has as much care that this sacrament of the New Testament should not be defiled as He had that the temple, altar, sacrifices, and feasts of old should be kept pure. Unclean persons were very strictly forbidden of old to come near. So these who are thus unclean by allowed wickedness are no less strictly to approach to the ordained sacred signs of the body and blood of Christ.

(2) Persons ought to examine whether or not it is their serious resolution to avoid all sin and live in obedience to all known commands as long as he lives, whether he now is in the practice of any known ways of sinning or not. Yet if he has a design of sinning hereafter, or if he doesn't explicitly design it, yet if he stands ready to commit sin as occasions offer, not having any resolutions against some, having never come to any determination of mind, of truly endeavoring to do everything that he ought to do, and of avoiding whatever he ought not to do, he is not fit to come to the sacrament, as will evidently appear presently.

Therefore persons, before they presume to come to the sacrament of the Lord's Supper, ought to examine themselves strictly as to this matter, whether that is their determination to avoid as long as they live all known sins, and to set themselves to walk in a way of obedience.

(3) But persons should particularly examine themselves before they come to the Lord's Supper whether or not they don't entertain a spirit of hatred or envy or revenge towards their neighbor. If a man has such a spirit towards any of his brethren and doesn't disallow it, but from time to time acts upon it, maintains such a spirit and disposition towards him, and gives vent to it, it renders him unfit to attend the sacrament of the Lord's Supper. And if he doesn't first draw up a resolution to lay it by and no more to allow it, he eats and drinks unworthily. Such a spirit in a man renders a man unfit and makes the ordinance void to him in the same manner as having leaven in a house rendered the Passover void. Leaven typified any wickedness, but especially malice and hatred. It fitly represented this by reason of its sourness. And the apostle calls malice "leaven," and directs us to keep the Christian feast without this leaven as they formerly kept the Passover without leaven. 1 Corinthians 5:8: "Therefore let us keep the feast not with old leaven, neither with the leaven of malice and wickedness." Here both wickedness in general, or any wicked practice, and malice in particular are mentioned as being in the Christian feast as malice was of old in the Jewish feast of the Passover.

Persons therefore should particularly examine themselves whether or not they have forgiven their enemies and those who have done them any hurt so as to allow no wishing of any hurt to them, and especially so as never to design to do anything to gratify a vengeful disposition towards them.

If men have quarrels one with another they should see

to it to put an end to 'em before they come to the Lord's Supper. If they come together to the Table of the Lord, maintaining their quarrels one with another and indulging a contentious spirit, a spirit of hatred, they eat and drink unworthily, whether they have any sincere disposition and desire to these things that are the main designs and ends, profession and benefits.

(4) Persons ought to examine themselves what it is they aim at in coming to the Lord's Supper, whether any of those ends for which the ordinance was appointed are what they aim at in coming, or whether it is only and altogether something else that Christ had no respect to in appointing it. The ordinance was appointed for the spiritual good of the partakers. If those therefore who come don't seek that in it, and 'tis not any desire of their spiritual good or from any conscientious regard to God's command that they come, but only for some by-end, some temporal advantage or credit, or merely that their children may not lie under the disgrace of being unbaptized, they eat and drink unworthily.

Thus did the Corinthians of whom the apostle speaks in the text. What moved them to come to the sacrament was not that they might commemorate Christ's death according to His institution, or that they might obtain spiritual good, but to nourish their bodies and gratify their sensitive appetite, not discerning the Lord's body.

3. Persons should examine themselves with respect to those things so that they may not eat and drink damnation to themselves. They who come with this unfitness or in this unworthy manner, all the while living in known sins or having never truly resolved against living in such sins, and har-

boring a spirit of hatred and ill will to their brethren, or aiming at nothing else but only some by-end perfectly depart from the design of the ordinance. They eat and drink judgment to themselves, that is to say, their eating and drinking does but the more expose them to eternal damnation and seals that damnation.

Those who worthily partake eat and drink eternal life, that is, their eating and drinking will be profitable to their souls, will tend to their salvation, and the promise of eternal life is sealed to them. But those who eat and drink unworthily eat and drink their own damnation, that is, by their eating and drinking they do greatly expose themselves to damnation and seal their own damnation, and that for the following reasons:

REASON 1. Because coming after such a manner is a horrid contempt of the ordinance and the things signified in it. To come and pretend to eat Christ's body and blood, and to dare to allowedly continue in the meantime their wicked practices, and to bring them into the presence of Christ, to the communion of His body and blood, shows a great contempt of it.

If a person should be invited to a prince's table, and should willfully and allowedly come with his garments all over defiled with ordure, it would show a great contempt of the prince and what that person was invited to. So it shows a great contempt of the ordinance and of Jesus Christ and His body and blood to improve it only for some temporal design and aim. Such persons are guilty of the body and blood of the Lord; they make themselves mere murderers of Christ.

Those who stood by when Christ was crucified and

showed that they made a light matter of it, and had treated the body of Christ when dying as dead contemptuously and with indignity, it might justly be imputed to 'em as partaking in His murder. So those who contemptuously treat those symbols of the body of Christ slain and His blood shed, why, they make themselves guilty of the body and blood of the Lord, that is, of murdering Him.

There are two ways of eating and drinking the body and blood of Christ. One is eating and drinking for spiritual food and nourishment, as the worthy partakers do; and another is eating the body and drinking the blood of Christ as a wild beast eats his prey. They do, as it were, drink the blood of Christ out of a murderous bloodthirstiness; they eat His flesh as Job says the men of his tabernacle said of him on whom they longed to be revenged. Job 31:31: "O that we had of his flesh." And this is to eat and drink as the murderers of Christ might be metaphorically said to eat the flesh and drink the blood of Christ, that is, a prey to their malice.

Unworthy partakers are partakers with those murderers; they are guilty of the body and blood of the Lord; they eat and drink their own damnation because they therein expressed such a contempt of that which is their only remedy from damnation, the body and blood of Jesus Christ. They who in eating and drinking receive and embrace Jesus Christ eat and drink because they receive the Savior as their salvation; but they who in eating and drinking do but trample on Christ and, as it were, spit in His face, eat and drink their damnation because they cast this indignity upon the only means of their salvation.

REASON 2. There is the most horrid dissimulation and

mockery. Persons, when they come into the church, make promises. And every participation in this ordinance is the most solemn renewal and sealing of those promises possible; for this ordinance is a seal on both parts. Christ sets His seal by the institution and by the action of the minister, His representative, at the ordinance; and men set their seal. And what a horrible piece of mockery is it to engage and promise explicitly at owning the covenant, and so exceeding solemnly at the partaking, and all the while never so much as seriously to purpose any such thing. And much more when they actually at the same time do live allowedly in things directly contrary to the gospel, contrary to the holy religion of Christ. They go on in known wickedness, things that they know Christ hates and has forbidden; they go on in the indulgences of their filthy lusts and come away from them and pretend, like saints, to commemorate Christ's death and to eat His flesh and drink His blood, and give themselves up to Christ, and then go from the Table of God to their old courses again is to come with malice and envy and to pretend to have great respect to the dying love of Christ, to use the bruising of His body and the shedding of His blood for the remission of our sins, to pretend to love and friendship for the family—if any eat the Passover with leaven, they eat and drink condemnation to themselves.

USE. Let this doctrine warn all persons carefully to examine themselves before they come to the Lord's Supper so that they don't seal their own damnation. If you would, as it were, consign yourself over to Satan, be careful; and if there are any who belong to this church who have hitherto neglected this duty of self-examination before they come, let them no more neglect it. And if there are any who have not taken up a resolution, any who live in any allowed sin, let them by no means approach nor partake till they have set upon self-examination. If you find yourself unfit in these respects, it won't excuse you from coming; your wickedness doesn't excuse you. Though it is true, if you will continue, you had much better stay away than come, but the end of examination is that you may amend before you come.

If there are any now about to approach who are going on in any of these mentioned ways, I forewarn them in the name of Jesus Christ not to presume to touch till they have taken up a resolution to stop. If you live in any known way of wickedness, don't come here to eat and drink damnation to yourselves.

7

The Spiritual Blessings of the Gospel Are Fitly Represented By a Feast

"Then said He unto him, 'A certain man made a great
supper and bade many.' " Luke 14:16

Christ, wherever He was and in whatever company, was wont to take opportunities to deliver heavenly instructions to teach men those things that pertained to their salvation. Upon every occasion He would introduce some divine discourse, as is easy to observe by anyone who takes notice of the history of His life.

Our text is some of His table discourse that He uttered upon occasion of being invited to a feast at one of the principal of the Pharisees houses. As He sat at meat, He took occasion first to rebuke the pride that He observed in the guests choosing the highest seats, and tells them that "he that exalteth himself shall be abased, and he that humbleth himself shall be exalted." And then He takes occasion to instruct His host not only to invite his brethren and kinsmen, his rich neighbor for his honor's sake, or expecting to be recompensed by being invited again, but to invite the poor, the maimed, the base, and the blind who needed relief and who could not recompense him.

They could not bid him to a feast of theirs, but he would be recompensed at the resurrection of the just, intimating that he would be rewarded by being invited to feast with the saints then.

As He said this, one of them that sat at meal with them said, "Blessed is he that shall eat bread in the kingdom of God." The Jews understood no other by the kingdom of God than the kingdom of the Messiah, as you have often heard. And they had this notion of the resurrection that when the Messiah came and the kingdom of God began that the saints of their nation would rise and so would be partakers of the happiness of the times of the Messiah. And that is the reason that when Christ told the Pharisee that if he invited the poor he would be blessed, for he would be rewarded at the resurrection of the just; for they could not invite him to a feast again, but he would feast at the resurrection. He consented to what Christ said, that they are indeed blessed that shall eat bread in this Messiah's kingdom when the just shall rise. Then Christ speaks the parable that begins with our text, comparing the blessings of the kingdom of God to a feast, and representing the freeness of the invitation to it and men's various receptions of the invitation.

The man who made the feast represents God or Jesus Christ; the feast itself represents the blessed provision that God has made for men's souls. Under the gospel, 'tis called a supper because it was their manner in those times to have all their feasts and entertainments at night. Therefore it is that the sacrament of Christ's body and blood is called a supper, and we read of Christ standing at the door and knocking, saying, "If any man hear My voice and open the door, I will come in and sup with him and He with Me' " (Revelation 3:20).

DOCTRINE. The spiritual blessings of the gospel are fitly represented by a feast.

God has wonderfully laid Himself out to make provision for the souls of fallen men. He contrived it from all eternity, and He has been preparing it from the beginning of time. Wonderful has been the cost that God has been at to provide for us; and this provision we find very often in Scripture compared to a feast that God has made for us. Thus the Prophet Isaiah, speaking of gospel times, prophesies in Isaiah 25:6: "And in this mountain shall the Lord of hosts make unto all people a feast of fat things." So we read in Proverbs 9:2 of wisdom's killing her beasts, mingling her wine, and furnishing her table. So when the prodigal son returned, they killed the fatted calf and feasted him and feasted with him.

This is the principle that was aimed at by the ceremonial feasts of the Old Testament, such as the feast of the Passover, the Feast of Tabernacles, and the Feast of Ingathering. An abundance of the occasional feasts they had were typical of the great gospel feast.

In this feast God is the Host; 'tis He who makes the provision and invites the guests. Sinners are the invited guests; believers are those who accept the invitation; and Jesus Christ, with His benefits that He purchased by His obedience and death, and which He communicates by His Spirit, is the entertainment. This is the meat and drink. Christ gives Himself for the life of the world. He is slain so that we may, as it were, eat His flesh and drink His blood. As the sacrifices of old were slain, and then that which was not burnt was eaten, thus considered, God the Father is the Host and Christ is the entertainment. Believers, as they live a life of faith, do, as it were, feed upon Christ Jesus. They live upon Him. He is their daily bread.

But if we consider these blessings of Christ's purchase that He invites us to accept, and that He communicates by His Spirit—such as sanctification, spiritual knowledge, and manifestation of God's favor, peace of conscience, joy in the Holy Ghost, and the exercises of holiness in good works—so Christ is the Host and the Holy Spirit is the entertainment. This is that water that Christ gives so that he who drinks shall never thirst, but it shall be in him a well of water springing up into everlasting life.

The faith, love, and hope that a believer exercises answers to the accepting of the invitation of those who are invited to a feast, and their coming to it and sitting at God's table and eating and drinking those good things with which He entertains them. But we shall show in some particular instances how gospel provision is well represented by a feast.

1. In the expensiveness of gospel blessings. As feasts are expensive and are provided at the expense of the host, so the provision that God has in the gospel made for our souls is exceedingly expensive. But we have it for nothing; it costs us nothing, but it cost God a great deal. Fallen men can't be feasted but at vast expense; we are by sin sunk infinitely low into the lowest depths of misery and want, and our famishing souls could not be provided for except under infinite expense.

All that we have from God for the salvation, support, and nourishment of our souls cost Him exceedingly dearly. Never were any feasted at so dear a rate as believers; when they eat and drink, it is a thousand times more costly than what they eat at the tables of princes that is far-fetched and dearly bought. Every crumb of bread that they eat and every drop of wine that they drink are more costly than so much gold or gems. God purchased it at no less a rate than with the blood of His only and infinitely dear Son. That holiness, that favor, that peace and joy that they have was bought with the heart's blood of the Son of God, His precious life. He made His soul an offering. Christ Jesus obtained this provision by victory. He was obliged to fight for it, as it were, up to His knees in blood so that He might obtain it; yea, He waded through a sea of blood to get it for us.

2. As the guests are freely invited to a feast, so sinners are freely invited to partake of gospel blessings. However much the provision has cost God, He requires nothing of us for it. Alas, what would we do if it were required of us to buy those dainties at our own cost? They can't be purchased with money. They cannot be gotten for gold; neither shall silver be weighed for the price thereof. This provision cannot be valued with the gold of Ophir, with the precious onyx or this sapphire; the gold and the crystal cannot equal it, and the exchange of it shall not be for jewels of fine gold. No mention shall be made of coral or quartz or pearls (Job 28:15–19). Alas, what can we do towards purchasing it? What is all our righteousness to purchase such heavenly dainties?

No, we can't purchase it; any price that we can offer is as insufficient to buy it, as our power is insufficient to create a world. And there is no need of our endeavoring such an impossible thing as purchasing this feast. We are freely invited. God will show the abundance of His divine liberality in the bestowment of it. It is to have most abject thoughts of God and of gospel blessings to imagine that God would sell them to us for our righteousness.

God invites all freely. Thus we read in our context that those who were poor, those who were in the highways and hedges, who were invited to this great supper, such as had nothing to pay, and such as did not pretend to it, it was with such that His house was filled and by such was His feast eaten. In Isaiah 55, all who thirst are invited to come and buy wine and milk without money and without price. Here we have the gospel invitation. They are very generally either to food or drink, as it is here. So it is in John 7:37: "If any man thirst, let him come unto Me and drink." Revelation 22:17: "And the Spirit and the bride say, 'Come,' and let him that heareth say, 'Come,' and let him that is athirst come, and whosoever will, let him take the water of life freely."

We are so freely invited to this feast that there is no other condition required of us in order to our partaking of this feast but accepting the invitation and sitting down at the table and eating and drinking. Proverbs 9:2–5: "Wisdom hath killed her beasts; she hath also mingled her wine. She hath also furnished her table. She hath sent forth her maidens. She crieth upon the highest places of the city, 'Whoso is simple, let him turn in hither.' As for him that wanteth understanding, she saith unto him, 'Come, eat of my bread and drink of the wine which I have mingled.' "

And in Revelation 3:20 Christ promises that He will

come in and sup with us, and we shall sup with Him if we only hear His voice and open the door.

3. The provision God has made for us in the gospel is fitly represented by a feast because it nourishes the soul as food does the body. Christ Jesus, as applied by the Spirit of God in our enlightening effectual calling and sanctification, is the only nourishment of the soul. It was He who was represented by the manna the children of Israel ate in the wilderness. It was He who was signified by the sacrifices, who is called the bread of God (Leviticus 21:6). John 6:48: "I am the bread of life."

Receiving Christ and His benefits is often called eating in the Old and New Testaments. And this provision is called bread in many places. The grace of Christ Jesus nourishes the soul; it gives life and strength to it. Before the soul receives this grace it is dead. In this it does more than bread does to the body; bread does but preserve the life of the body and revives it when weakened and languishing. But this heavenly food revives men when dead, and it also continues the life of the soul. The soul, after it is revived would die again were it not for the continuance of a supply of grace and spiritual nourishment. It strengthens the soul as food does the body. The soul in its natural condition is a poor, feeble, languishing thing, having no strength; but the grace of Christ makes it strong and vigorous. And this spiritual nourishment makes the soul to grow as food does the body. The supplies of the Spirit of God increase the life and vigor of the soul, increases the understanding, increases holy inclinations and affections. As bodily nourishment increases, all the members of the body make a proportionate growth of every part.

Thus Christ is called our life (Revelation 2:7), and the Spirit of Christ is called the water of life (Revelation 22:1), and we are said to grow up in Christ Jesus and to be strong in the Lord and in the power of His might.

4. The spiritual provision of the gospel is well represented because of the excellency of it. We call those meals feasts where the provision is what excels ordinary food. The provision that God has made for our souls in Christ is exceedingly excellent; 'tis of the most noble kind, and is that which is to nourish the nobler part of man, that is, his soul, and that which is most suitable, proper nourishment, that which tends above all that can be conceived of to give the soul the most excellent life and the most excellent satisfaction, which is evident by what has been already said about the costliness of it, its being what cannot be gotten for gold. Doubtless that food that cost the Son of God His blood and life is pure dainties when it is procured; and it is everywhere represented as the richest and most noble and excellent food. It is called the bread of heaven and angels' food (Psalm 105:40). So we are invited in Isaiah 55 not to spend money for that which is not bread, or to labor for that which does not satisfy, but to come to Christ to eat that which is good so that our souls may delight themselves in fatness.

So this feast in Isaiah 25:6 is called a feast of fat things, of wines on the lees, of fat things full of marrow, of wines on the lees well refined. This feast is a royal feast, the feast of a king. So we read in the parable in Matthew 22 of a certain king who made a feast. Christ tells His spouse that He had laid up for her all manner of pleasant fruits, new and old. Those dainties must be the sweetest and what give exceeding satisfaction and happiness to the soul, for the same kind that Christ Himself is, as it were, delighted with they are, what satisfy Him. Therefore He tells His disciples of drinking the fruit of the vine new with them in His Father's kingdom. That which now makes Christ happy in heaven is the same sort of wine with which He satisfies thirsty souls on earth, and will satisfy them in heaven.

5. Gospel provision is well compared to a feast by reason of the abundance and variety of it. There is every kind of blessing for our souls provided in the gospel that we need, so that we may want nothing at all, but may have every regular appetite and desire satisfied, and we may be made complete. There is that which suits all dispositions and tempers, provided they are suitable and not sinful. There is every kind of thing dispensed in Christ that tends to make us excellent and amiable, and every kind of thing that tends to make us happy. There is that which shall fill every faculty of the soul, and in a great variety. What a glorious variety is there for the entertainment of the understanding. How many glorious objects are set forth, most worthy to be meditated upon and understood. There are all the glorious attributes of God and the beauties of Jesus Christ, manifold wonders to be seen in the way of salvation, the glories of heaven and the excellency of Christian graces. And there is a glorious variety for satisfying the will; there are pleasures, riches, and honors. There are all things desirable or lovely; there is various entertainment for the affections, for love, for joy, for desire and hope. The blessings are innumerable.

And then, besides this, each kind is in great abundance; there is an inexhaustible fountain of blessings. Every kind of dainty is in inexhaustible plenty. Therefore it is called a river of water of life, rivers of pleasure forevermore. Here the soul manifests itself abundantly without danger of spending the provision. Therefore Christ says to His people, "Eat, O friends; drink ye drink abundantly, O beloved" (Song of Solomon 5:1). There is no such thing as excess in our taking this spiritual food; there is no such virtue as temperance in spiritual feasting.

6. The measure of love of Jesus Christ and Christians, and of Christians among themselves, is represented by the friendship of those who feast together. Thus Abimelech and Isaac made a covenant (Genesis 26:30) of love and friendship. So it is from the wonderful love of Jesus Christ that sinners are called to this feast, and that He has provided such a feast for them at so dear a rate.

This love is without a parallel, and all those who accept the invitation, who are truly His guests, their hearts are possessed with a spirit of true love to Christ Jesus. They love Him above all. He is to them the chief of ten thousands and altogether lovely. There is a great love between Christ and His guests. He and they are one even as the Father is in Him and He in the Father. There is the nearest union and a holy friendship between Christ and believers; they are Christ's dear ones, His jewels, and Christ is that jewel, their "pearl of great price."

And so there is mutual love among the guests. Believers are united in heart one to another. Therefore all men know that they are Christ's disciples in that they have love one to another. They are all united under their Host, under their head Christ Jesus, with whom they sit at His table.

Therefore Christ says, "Eat, O friends" (Song of Solomon 5:1). They are Christ's friends, and friends one to another.

7. The communion of saints is represented by a feast. The word "communion," as it is used in Scripture, signifies a common partaking of some good. Thus we read of the communion of the body of Christ, and the communion of the blood of Christ, that is, the common partaking of His body and blood. Therefore, as in a feast they all have communion in the same fare with the host and with the other guests, so Christians have communion with Jesus. They partake of the same Spirit, of the same holiness and the same happiness. They are members of Christ's body and partake of the same life with the Head. They are branches in Him and partake of the same sap and nourishment with the vine.

Christ and believers are partakers of the same Spirit. Christ has the Spirit not by measure, and they have the same Spirit by measure. Christ has all fullness of grace in Him and believers have grace for grace. Christ eats of the same feast with believers and He eats with them; they sit with the King at His table (Song of Solomon 1:12). Christ tells us that, if we will open the door, He will come in and sup with us and we with Him. Christ sat with His disciples at His first sacrament, which signifies that He always has communion with them in the same spiritual blessings. In Song of Solomon 5:1, we read first of Christ eating, and then commanding His friends to eat: "I am come into my garden, my sister, my spouse. I have gathered my myrrh with my spice. I have eaten my honeycomb with my honey. I have drunk my wine with my milk. Eat, O friends." And believers are also partakers of the same glory with Jesus

Christ: they shall sit with Him on His throne.

Believers in the gospel feast also have communion one with another. They all partake of that one bread. They have one Lord, one faith, one baptism. All drink into one Spirit, are all united together by partaking of the same influence of the same Head. 'Tis one Spirit that unites them all so that they make but one body.

8. Last, this well represents the joy of Christianity. Feasts are made upon joyful occasions and for the manifestations of joy (Ecclesiastes 10:19). A feast is made for laughter. Christians in the participation and communion of gospel benefits have joy unspeakable and full of glory, a sweeter delight than any this world affords. We are invited in that forecited place, Isaiah 55, to come so that our souls may delight themselves in fatness. When the prodigal son returned they killed the fatted calf and made a feast and sang and danced and made merry. This represents the joy there is in a sinner, and concerning him, when he comes to Christ.

This spiritual feast is compared to a wedding feast; so was the feast spoken of in our text a wedding feast, as appears by the same parable as it is in Matthew 22. Being in the kingdom of heaven is like a certain king who made a marriage for his son. And so it is in Revelation 19:9: "Blessed are they which shall be called to the marriage supper of the Lamb."

Because of the joyfulness of gospel blessings, they are compared to a banquet as well as a feast. Song of Solomon 2:4: "He brought me into the banqueting house."

Thus we have shown how gospel benefits of the gospel are fitly compared to a feast. Indeed, all representations are but shadows.

Application

1. Hence we learn the wisdom of Christ in appointing
the sacrament of the Lord's Supper. The Lord's Supper is
a representation of this spiritual gospel feast. It is very suitable to the gospel state of the church—the state wherein
God's grace in providing for souls is so abundantly manifested and this spiritual provision so plentifully bestowed—
that there should be a feast appointed and observed in the
church showing forth the spiritual feast that God has provided in Jesus Christ for our souls with such great expense,
and to signify and seal the covenant with friendship between God and His people. And in this ordinance is represented the great cost that God has been at to provide this
feast for us in the representation of the breaking of the
body and shedding of the blood of Jesus Christ in order
that we might have our spiritual blessings by the body and
blood of Christ; and Christ did, as it were, submit himself
to death that He might give His body and blood to be our
meat and drink, that we might have such food as would
nourish and satisfy our souls in this sacrament. We have
this represented to us.

How well is that great love there is between Christ and
His disciples signified, and the covenant between God and
them, when Abimelech and Isaac made a feast to seal it
(Genesis 26:30). We have been at enmity with God; we
have been God's enemy, and we have made God our enemy. We are naturally the objects of His wrath; but in
Christ He is reconciling sinners to Himself. And in Him

God loves us with an exceeding love. And, to manifest and confirm this amity and love, God has appointed this feast wherein God does, as it were, invite us to His own table and sits down with us. He receives us into His house and family and feasts us at His own table.

How well is the communion between Christ and believers signified by this ordinance, for as has been said, Christ was not only with His disciples at the first sacrament, but He sits with His people in every sacrament. Here is a signification how we partake of the same spiritual dainties that satisfy and delight the soul of our Savior.

And by this sacrament is well signified the union, love, and communion of saints. They feast together, friends and brethren, members of the same love and thirst who drink of the same spirit. They are of the same family, and eat of the same spiritual meat and drink.

God's wisdom is to be seen in the choices of the elements. The bread, which is the staff of life, best signifies that spiritual life and nourishment that we have in Christ, and that best signifies the body of Christ, that bread that came down from heaven, and the wine, that best signifies the spiritual joy and delight that the church has in Jesus Christ. Those are the same elements that were the meat offering and the drink offering under the law, and the same that Melchizedek, that great type of Christ, gave to Abraham. These signified the same spiritual blessings that bread and wine do in the sacrament (Genesis 14:18).

2. Hence we learn what exceedingly great reason we have to admire the grace of God towards us, that He should so lay Himself out to provide such a feast for our souls. God hasn't provided this feast for those who are

rich, who are able to recompense Him by inviting Him again, nor for them who are able to make any recompense at all, but those who are poor and have nothing to pay. We were in a famishing, miserable condition when the King invited us to the marriage feast of His Son, and, not only so, but to be His bride.

God did not make this feast for those who were excellent and worthy to be invited to such a royal feast, but for those who were filthy, who were loathsome creatures clothed in rags, or rather naked and defiled with filth. He did not invite those who were happy already, but poor beggars who were scattered, wandering in the highways and dwelling under hedges, those who were halt and lame and blind. Such all naturally are, but God sends forth His messengers and calls many such to His houses, washes them from their filthiness, clothes them with white raiment, adorns them with robes as king's children, and makes them to sit down at His table. Oh, what reason we have to admire the wonderful grace of God herein!

3. I would take occasion to invite the poor, the maimed, the halt, and the blind unto this feast (Luke 14:21). We read in the context that the man who made the feast sent forth his servant into the highway and hedges to compel them to come in. And we read in Proverbs 9 that wisdom had killed her beast and mingled her wine and furnished her table. She sent forth her maiden to say, "Whoso is simple, let him turn in hither," which signifies gospel ministers. We are therefore sent forth in the name of Christ to invite you to come to this feast; therefore you have sufficient warrant to come from this invitation. And you may be sure that you shall be accepted.

You who are natural men are in a very sorrowful, doleful condition. Your poverty and misery are beyond expression. You are more miserable than if you were beggars in the highway, more than if you were perishing with hunger and thirst, more than if you were maimed, blind, and lame. You are in a miserable, abject state. You are more loathsome than a beggar clothed with rags and full of sores.

Doesn't it move you at all, therefore, what provision God has made for you, what glorious entertainment He has provided for you? Have you no heart to accept the invitation? Is it not worth the while to be taken from hedges and dunghills, and to be clothed with wrought gold and jewels, to dwell in a palace and sit at a prince's table? Is it not worth the while to accept any invitation to come to the marriage supper of the Lamb? Blessed and happy are they who enter in with God into the marriage. Yea, is not she blessed who shall be the bride, the Lamb's wife, to whom it shall be granted to be clothed in fine linen, clean and white, which is the righteousness of the saints (Revelation 19:8).

You know not how sweet and satisfying the meat and drink of this feast is, and what abundance and variety there is. If you did, you would need no compelling to come; the sense of it would be wings to your feet. You know not what friendship, what communion, what love and joy there are at God's table. Taste and see that the Lord is gracious. Put off your filthy garments; wash yourself from your filthiness; accept the white raiment Christ offers you. Go to Christ and enter with Him into His chambers. Sit down with Him in His feasting and banqueting house.

Here consider two things:

1. You are now invited, but you know not that He may cease to invite you. You don't know but Christ may give you over in a very little while; now the door is open, but if you stay much longer, the door will be shut and you don't know how soon. And if you stay till then before you accept that invitation you will be sorry for it afterwards. You'll come and knock at the door and say, "Lord, Lord, open to us," and there is nobody who will open the door for you. If you begin to make excuses and won't come when you may, you can't come when you will. How was it with them who began to make excuses in our text, beginning with verse 17: "And he sent forth his servants at supper time to say to them that were bidden, 'Come, for all things are now ready.' And they all with one consent began to make excuse." He said afterwards in verse 24, "None of those men which were bidden shall taste of my supper."

2. This feast is an eternal feast. You aren't invited to feast daintily for once, and then to return to your old beggarly, famished condition you were in before, but this royal provision is to be your perpetual entertainment. You may live upon such food forever and ever; you shall enter into the house of God and you shall go no more out. You have been hungry and thirsty in times past, but if you come to this gospel feast you shall hunger and thirst no more. Revelation 7:16: "They shall hunger no more nor thirst anymore." John 6:35: "He that cometh to Me shall never hunger and he that believeth on Me shall never thirst." At God's right hand there are pleasures forevermore. There you may always eat and drink, and always be

satisfied, and yet never be glutted. You may eat and drink abundantly and never be in danger of excesses.

That this may not hereafter be the case with you to see others, attend these directions:

DIRECTION 1. You must choose the kingdom of God for your portion. That so many fail of entering into the kingdom and shall stand without as rejected when they shall see so many others entering in is not because the terms of admittance are hard. God only requires that men should choose that kingdom for their portion and the happiness of it for their happiness, and then they shall have it. They shall enter in and sit down with other saints. God leaves them to their choice. God would not give the kingdom of heaven to them who don't much value it, who don't set their hearts upon it, but would rather have the world, than have them who don't account the happiness of it worth much seeking, who treat it with neglect and prefer the vanities of the world before it with a great deal more earnestness and more affection.

God doesn't mean to bestow the kingdom of heaven upon any but those who prize and value it. God doesn't set forth such a glorious gift as the kingdom of heaven to be slighted and trampled on as those who throw pearls before swine. God would not command this inestimable happiness and glory upon men against their wills. God is freely willing that man should have it, but only He would have them sensible of the worth and value of it, that they should prize and set their hearts upon it. God would not give this precious jewel to be set below the dust of the earth. He won't give it to those men who prefer their worldly self before it.

The kingdom of heaven is a thing of infinitely more value than all worldly things, and they who prefer eathly things before it shall not have it. But all that choose it for their portion have a right and title to it. God gives it to 'em freely.

They who at the Day of Judgment shall be thrust out and shall see others admitted now indeed would gladly enter in. Now they wish and long for entrance. But why were they not more concerned about it when they might have had it when God offered it to 'em, as He does to gospel sinners over and over again? But then they concerned themselves little about it; they sold the kingdom of heaven for pleasure, a little worldly gain, a few trivial worldly vanities.

Therefore be entreated, you who yet have the offer of the kingdom of heaven, now to make choice of it. Be content to sell all for this pearl of great price. Matthew 13:44–46: "The kingdom of heaven is like unto a treasure hid in a field which, when a man hath found, he hideth and for joy thereof goeth and selleth all that he hath and buyeth that field. Again the kingdom of heaven is like unto a merchant man seeking goodly pearls who, when he had found one pearl of great price, he went and sold all that he had and bought it."

As long as you set your heart, your honor, on estates or pleasures more than upon the kingdom of heaven, you may be sure that you never shall have the possession of it. You must prize this blessedness above any worldly blessing.

Your heart must be most upon it. It must be your portion. There is no such thing as your choosing two portions, choosing the world for a portion and the kingdom of God for a portion too. Matthew 6:24: "No man can serve two masters." But if you once are brought to renounce the world, to choose your happiness here, so that this shall be the happiness you most relish, have a greatest appetite to, most earnest desires after and do chiefly pursue, there is no doubt but that when those multitudes are flocking from the ease and from sitting down in the Kingdom of God, you will be admitted amongst 'em.

DIRECTION 2. Labor to get your soul clothed with Christ's righteousness. At the Day of Judgment, none will be admitted but those who shall be found having on Christ's righteousness. All others who clothe themselves with their own righteousness shall be stripped naked and shall see their shame.

Many trust in their own righteousness; they flatter themselves with hope of admittance through that, but men who are found clothed with no other righteousness shall be admitted. Men's righteousness that they think makes them look lovely in the sight of God will appear in that day in the sight of all, and even in their own sight, to be but a most filthy, wretched covering and that which renders most deformed and abominable.

But at that day everyone who appears shining with the white and beautiful robes of Christ's righteousness upon him, in whatever quarter or region of the earth he is, why, Christ will readily own him. He will soon be conducted by angels into the kingdom of God and to a throne of glory at Christ's right hand; he shall have abundant entrance administered to him into Christ's joy; he shall be received with great welcome, with great love and great joy.

Christ will by no means thrust forth any such as are

found clothed with His own righteousness; no, but He'll welcome him to his right hand. They who have the righteousness of Christ on haven't any clothing of their own making; they haven't any clothing that any creature could make for them. They have that clothing that God speaks of in Revelation 19:8: "And to her was granted that she should be arrayed in fine linen, clean and white." It is not a garment of human workmanship, but of the workmanship of Christ Jesus, the eternal wisdom of God. They who have Christ's righteousness on them have Christ's own robes upon them. The beauty of those robes will appear so great, and will thus appear so lovely therein, that it will provide for them the most ready and easy admittance. None will incline to shut out those who shine forth with such a glorious beauty, who have the beautiful righteousness of Christ Jesus upon them.

The righteousness of Christ is a most excellent righteousness and acceptable to God the Father. The obedience was perfect. He obeyed at a wonderful expense and self-denial. He was obedient unto death, even the death of the cross. His obedience was of infinite value because the Son expressed in it an infinite love for God the Father, whom He obeyed.

This righteousness that is thus excellent will doubtless prove a ready admittance for you for it even merits it. If you are clothed with this righteousness, you may challenge an entrance as your right. You have that righteousness. Your own estate, the kingdom of heaven is not at all too great a reward, for 'tis not a whit more than a reward equal to the excellency and desert of the righteous. 'Tis but justice that you should enter into the kingdom of heaven if your soul is clothed with the righteousness of Christ. This is the price with which Christ purchased that kingdom, and the price is an adequate price; the price is of as much worth and value as the thing purchased. So, if you have on the righteousness of Christ, you are in Christ worthy of the kingdom of heaven and deserve to be admitted by a merit of condignity—and as such will doubtless be admitted. It is impossible but that God should be willing that you should be admitted to sit down in the kingdom of heaven if you are clothed with the righteousness of Christ. 'Tis the righteousness of Him who is to be the Judge. Christ is appointed the Judge of the world. He is to admit to eternal life whom He pleases, whom He thinks fit. And how can any suppose that He will reject those who are clothed with His own righteousness?

Therefore let this be your aim, that you may get your soul clothed with that righteousness. And to that end, seek that you may be made sensible how destitute you are of righteousness in yourself; seek that you may see your own emptiness and filthiness and undone, desperate state as to anything that is in and of yourself. Seek faith in Jesus Christ. All who believe in Him and trust in Him for salvation shall be clothed with His righteousness.

DIRECTION 3. If you would not be shut out of the kingdom of heaven at the last day, when you see others entering in, labor that you may have Christ's mark set upon you, and that is that you be of Christ's spirit and temper and of a Christ-like behavior. Christ does, as it were, set His mark upon His own flock whereby He distinguishes them from others. The servants of God are sealed with God's seals and marks on their foreheads. Revelation

7:3: "Hurt not the earth nor the seas till you have sealed
the servants of our God in their foreheads." And again,
chapter 14:1: "And I looked, and lo, a Lamb stood on Mt.
Zion, and with him a hundred and forty and four thousand, having His Father's name written in their foreheads."

They who are found at the Day of Judgment with
Christ's mark on them shall doubtless be admitted, and
none else. This mark is being of a Christ-like spirit and
temper. When the soul is regenerated and its nature
changed, renewed, and sanctified, then has it Christ's
mark set; it is then made partaker of the divine nature; it is
changed into Christ's image (2 Corinthians 3:18). When a
person is converted and has his nature changed, he then
puts on Christ (Galatians 3:27). They become of a spirit
and disposition like His. They are partakers of His holy,
heavenly, meek, lowly, charitable, loving disposition and
behavior. Those graces are as a stamp on the soul, a seal
wherein is the name of Christ, in that that is an image of
His nature.

And then also their likeness to Christ begins to show itself, their Christ-like behavior; they follow Christ's example. The redeemed from among men are said to follow the
Lamb wherever He goes. They manifest that temper of
Christ in their behavior.

At the Day of Judgment men must be judged by their
works; and they whose works are Christian, which is the
same thing as Christ-like, shall be admitted as having
Christ's mark upon them. Labor therefore now, which is
the only opportunity to get this mark of Jesus Christ set
upon your soul. And then you will have an open entrance
into the kingdom of God, your Sovereign.

DIRECTION 4. Last, if you would enter the kingdom of heaven, be content while here to bear the cross. Christ tells us that, if we would be His disciples, we must take up our cross daily (Luke 9:23). Christ obtained the kingdom by enduring the cross, and so must we. The cross is the way to the crown; a way of having the cross is the straight and narrow way that leads to life. We must be content to bear the cross; that is to say, we must deny all our lusts and to bear all suffering for Christ's sake. We must pluck out right eyes and cut off right hands if we would not go to hell having two eyes and two hands.

The Christian life is a warfare, and the crown is promised only to those who overcome. If you therefore would have admittance, you must come. The reason so few will be admitted is that few will comply with the requirements. Be in those things conformed to Christ's death, and then you shall also be conformed to His resurrection and glorious exultation, as in Philippians 3:10–11.

8

Christians Have Communion With Christ

"God is faithful, by whom ye were called unto the fellowship of his Son Jesus Christ our Lord." 1 Corinthians 1:9

The apostle begins this epistle to the Corinthians by expressing to them his thankfulness to God on their behalf for the grace of God that was given them by Jesus Christ; and he proceeds in the fifth, sixth and seventh verses to enumerate some of the particular fruits of God's grace in them: "That in everything ye are enriched by Him in all utterance and in all knowledge, even as the testimony of Christ was confirmed in you; so that ye come behind in no gift, waiting for the coming of our Lord Jesus Christ." The last is their waiting for the coming of the Lord Jesus Christ, when they expected to receive the end and reward of the grace that God had given 'em.

And in the eighth and ninth verses, the apostle says something to encourage that expectation and confirm and establish their faith in the promise of the glorious reward that shall be bestowed on them when Christ shall appear. And lest they should fear that they should miss it by their falling away, he assures them (v. 8) that Christ will confirm them "unto the end, that ye may be blameless in the day of our Lord Jesus Christ."

And then, in our text, he shows them, first, upon what foundation they may be assured that they shall be so confirmed to the end and then have the reward bestowed on them, and that is the faithfulness of God. And then, second, he shows how God is obliged in faithfulness to keep them to the day of Christ, and then to reward them, in that He had called them to the fellowship of the Lord Jesus Christ. He had by the gospel invited and called them to an acceptance of Christ upon that encouragement and promise that if they would come to Him, they would have fellowship or communion with Christ and be partakers with Him in grace and glory. And by effectually calling them by His Spirit, He had enabled them to accept this gospel call and invitation, and so to perform the condition, and likewise had thereby given them fellowship with Christ already in part by their being partakers of His grace. This was an earnest of what was to come: they had not only God's invitation and promise, but also His pledge of this more perfect and complete fellowship with Christ. This last part of the verse is what we shall insist on at this time, and from this doctrine:

DOCTRINE: Christians have communion with Christ.

We shall examine:

1. What is meant by "communion" in the text and doctrine.

2. What communion with Christ that is that we are called to by the gospel.

3. How we are called by the gospel to communion with Christ.

1. What is meant by "communion." In one word, 'tis a common partaking of the same benefits in society. There are these two things meant by it: first, a common partaking of the same good; second, in that mutual society that arises from it.

First, that which is principally intended by "communion" or "fellowship" in Scripture is a common partaking of benefits. The word "communion" arises from *communis*, which signifies "common." And what is intended by "communion" is the having enjoyments in good things common between two and more. When any person partakes of an enjoyment or a blessing in common with another, or when he is a sharer with him in it, then he has communion or fellowship with him in a Scripture sense.

When we say that saints have communion with God, what is principally meant is that they are partakers with God of His holiness and happiness. So when we speak of the communion of saints, nothing else is meant but their common partaking of the same benefits of that gospel, as is represented in Ephesians 4:4-7, 11-13:

> There is one body and one Spirit, even as ye are called in one hope of your calling; one Lord, one faith, one baptism, one God and Father of all, who is above all, and through all, and in you all. But unto every one of us is given grace according to the measure of the gift of Christ. And He gave some, apostles; and some,

prophets; and some, evangelists; and some, pastors and teachers; for the perfecting of the saints, for the work of the ministry, for the edifying of the body of Christ: till we all come in the unity of the faith, and of the knowledge of the Son of God, unto a perfect man, unto the measure of the stature of the fullness of Christ.

So when we say that Christians have communion one with another at the Lord's table, the meaning of it is that they there partake in common of the same body and the same blood of Christ, they eat of the same spiritual meat and drink together of the same spiritual drink, and that by their partaking of the same elements, their common partaking of the same pains and benefits of Christ's death is signified.

It is this that is principally meant by everywhere in Scripture the word "fellowship" or "communion" (which are the same word in the original, *alm*). So it is in 1 Corinthians 10:16: "The cup of blessing which we bless, is it not the communion of the blood of Christ? And the bread which we break, is it not the communion of the body of Christ?" There can be no other sense of the expressions "communion of the blood" and "communion of the body" but Christians' common partaking of them.

So 'tis plain, 'tis to be understood, 2 Corinthians 8:4, "Praying us with much entreaty that we would receive the gift, and take upon us the fellowship of the ministering to the saints"; that is, that we would be sharers with others in that work. So Ephesians 3:8-9: "Unto me, who am less than the least of all saints, is this grace given, that I should

preach among the Gentiles the unsearchable riches of
Christ; and to make all men see what is the fellowship of
the mystery, which from the beginning of the world hath
been hid in God, who created all things by Jesus Christ."
And Philippians 1:5: "For your fellowship in the gospel
from the first day until now." And 1 John 1:3: "That which
we have seen and heard declare we unto you, that ye also
may have fellowship with us"; that is, plainly, "That ye may
be made acquainted with the same things that we are, and
might be partakers with us of the benefit of what we have
seen and heard."

So by the communion of the Holy Ghost, nothing else
is to be understood but a common partaking of the Holy
Ghost. Christians have the communion of the Holy Ghost,
that is, they are partakers together with Christ and one
with another of the same Spirit. Christ has the Spirit without measure, and believers are partakers of His Spirit; they
have of his fullness, for so they are partakers one with another of the same Spirit. As the apostle expresses it, they all
"drink into one Spirit" (1 Corinthians 12:13). And that is
meant by their having communion of the Holy Ghost.

And that is to be understood by the communion of the
Holy Ghost in that blessing of the apostle (2 Corinthians
13:14) that we use in dismissing our public assemblies. We
wish that Christians may have the grace of the Lord Jesus
Christ, and the love of God, and that they may be partakers of the Holy Ghost.

That is the reason that the phrase is varied when used
with respect to the Holy Ghost. We read of fellowship or
communion with the Father and with His Son Jesus Christ,
but not of communion with the Holy Ghost, but the

communion *of* the Holy Ghost; for that is the thing wherein they have fellowship or are partakers with the Father and with His Son Jesus Christ and with one another, that they have the communion or are partakers of the same Spirit.

And this is what is principally meant by the word "communion" in Scripture. I have been the more particular in explaining it because of the vulgar mistakes that some are under about it, and because I thought it fitting that the blessing used should be universally understood.

But yet, second, another thing that is secondarily understood by "communion" is that mutual society that arises from such a common partaking of benefits. A partaking together of the same enjoyments naturally begets mutual communication and society. And, indeed, this common partaking of the same things is the foundation of all society whatsoever: all friendly society either arises from such a common partaking or else is in order to it.

Where there are two or more having fellowship together in the same benefit, this naturally leads to mutual conversation. It begets love and friendship and a mutual intercourse, and this is also included in the meaning of the word "communion." Communion is not a partaking of the same benefit separately and ignorantly and unwillingly, but 'tis a common partaking of benefits in union and society.

'Tis a partaking joined with a friendly, sociable communication. This always goes before communion, and where there is a common partaking in union, there necessarily arises friendly communication and society.

But, however, this is not what is principally intended, but only in a secondary sense. 'Tis therefore a vulgar mistake that communion is nothing else but only society or conversation. To have communion with God, as many mistakenly understand it, is nothing else but to have spiritual conversation with God.

2. We are come now in the second place to show what communion with Christ it is that we are called to by the gospel.

First, saints have communion with Christ in being partakers with Him of His righteousness, of the benefit of His obedience and sufferings. Christ Himself as Mediator is gloriously rewarded for His obedience, and especially for His being obedient to death. He undertook it upon the encouragement of a reward. He "for the joy that was set before Him endured the cross, despising the shame, and is now set down at the right hand of the throne of God" (Hebrews 12:2). Philippians 2:8-9: "And being found in fashion as a man, He humbled Himself, and became obedient unto death, even the death of the cross. Wherefore God also hath highly exalted Him, and given Him a name which is above every name."

Believers are partakers with Him in His righteousness; they all have communion in the benefit and reward of it. As God accepted Christ and was well-pleased with Him for it, so He accepts and is well-pleased with believers for it also. As Christ is rewarded for it, so are believers rewarded with Him. Romans 5:19: "By the obedience of one," many are made righteous. He performed this righteousness as our Head, and Head and members are all together partakers of it.

So they are partakers with Him of the benefit of His sacrifice. Christ Himself, as our Surety, has the benefit of

His own sacrifice. He was justified by it. He took guilt upon Himself by His sufferings. He put it on Himself. He abolished it, and by His resurrection both He and we were justified. Thus Christ partakes with us of His own body and blood, which was signified by His eating with the disciples at sacrament.

Second, they have communion with Christ in His relation to the Father. Christ stands in the relation of a Son to God. He is His beloved. And believers, by virtue of their union to Him, also stand in the relation of sons. John 1:12: "But as many as received Him, to them gave He power to become sons of God, even to them that believe on His name." They are often called "the children of God." John 20:17: "I ascend to My Father, and your Father." And by virtue of this communion in relation, they have communion with Christ in the Father's love and delight. God loves them with a fatherly love, loves them as children, takes care of them. John 14:21: "He that loveth Me shall be loved of My Father." John 16:27: "For the Father Himself loveth you because ye have loved Me, and have believed that I came out from God."

And there is also intended in this a communion with Christ in His inheritance. As they are partakers with Christ in the relation of sonship, so by virtue of that they are partakers of the inheritance of sons. They are heirs along with Him. Romans 8:17: "And if children, then heirs; heirs of God, and joint-heirs with Christ."

Third, they have communion with Christ in partaking of the same Spirit. This is indeed the main thing wherein a believer's communion with Christ consists: they have the fellowship of the Spirit; they drink into the same Spirit with

Christ. 1 Corinthians 6:17: "He that is joined to the Lord is one Spirit." Those who are in Christ have the Spirit of Christ. Those who have not the Spirit of Christ are none of His.

Christ has the Spirit without measure. "God giveth not the Spirit by measure unto Him" (John 3:34). And of His fullness all believers receive, and grace for grace (John 1:16). He is full of the Spirit, and they receive of that fullness. He is full of grace, and they partake of His grace. They have grace for grace, that is, grace answerable to His grace. Christ has many graces, and He has no grace but that believers have one of the same kind to answer it; and so they have grace for grace.

Believers partake of Christ's Spirit just as the members of the body partake of the life of the head, or as the branches of a tree have the same sap with the body and root. Now by believers partaking of the same Spirit, they partake with Him in these following things:

(1) They partake with Him in divine knowledge. Christ, more than any other whatsoever, has the knowledge of God. He is in the bosom of the Father, and is perfectly acquainted with Him. John 8:55: "Ye have not known Him, but I know Him." And 10:15: "As the Father knoweth Me, even so know I the Father." And Matthew 11:27: "No man knoweth the Son but the Father; neither knoweth any man the Father save the Son, and he to whomsoever the Son will reveal Him."

And as Christ knows God Himself, so He gives the knowledge of Him to His disciples by His Spirit. Christ tells His disciples that the Comforter, when He is come, shall teach them all things (John 16:13-14). So Christ causes us with open face to behold "as in a glass the glory of the Lord" (2 Corinthians 3:18).

(2) They partake with Him in the same holy temper and disposition. They partake of the same disposition that Christ is of, as He is God; they are of a divine disposition. Therefore the Apostle Peter says in 2 Peter 1:4 that they are "partakers of the divine nature."

So they partake with Him in the same temper Jesus Christ expressed when on earth, the same holy and heavenly-minded, the same humble temper, the same love for God; the same mind is in them that was in Christ Jesus (Philippians 2:5). And especially when this holy temper is in exercise may a believer be said to have communion with Christ.

(3) By partaking of the same Spirit of Christ, they are also partakers of the same comfort and spiritual joy. The Spirit of Christ is therefore called "the Comforter."

As Christ rejoices in the love of the Father, so He gives to believers to have joy in God by His Spirit. They have joy in the Holy Ghost; they rejoice with joy unspeakable. John 17:13: "And now come I to Thee; and these things I speak in the world, that they may have my joy fulfilled in themselves."

That spiritual joy that believers have is Christ's joy. It is such a sort of joy as Christ rejoices with. They rejoice in the same things and rejoice in the same manner, and the same Spirit is the fountain of the joy of both; and they receive their joy from Christ by receiving of His Spirit.

So Christ gives His disciples His peace. John 14:27: "My peace I give unto you."

(4) And lastly, the saints have communion with Christ in glory. They shall partake of the same glory in heaven.

Christ is gone into heaven not as a private Person, but as our Head. He is gone to take possession of glory not only for Himself, but for all His. Christ's glory that God has advanced Him to is exceedingly great, without doubt; in what an exalted manner is it spoken of in Scripture. But they shall partake with Him as the wife partakes of the goods of her husband, and as the members partake with the head.

Christ will give them His glory. John 17:22: "And the glory which Thou gavest Me, have I given them."

They shall partake with Christ in the same glorious form. They shall shine forth as the sun with Him in the kingdom of His Father. They shall have the same sort of glory upon them. 1 John 3:2: "But this we know, that when we shall appear we shall be like Him; for we shall see Him as He is." 8:17: "If we suffer with Him, we shall also be glorified together."

As Christ will be in the presence of the Father, so shall those who are Christ's; as He shall enjoy the love of the Father, so shall those who are Christ's. They shall drink of the same river of pleasure that Christ shall. That was what Christ meant when He told His disciples that He would drink new wine with them in His Father's kingdom (Matthew 26:29).

They shall have communion with Christ in His rule and dominion. They shall sit down with Him on His throne. Revelations 3:21: "To him that overcometh I will grant to sit down with Me in My throne, even as I also overcame, and am set down with My Father in His throne."

And they shall have communion with Christ in His resurrection. As He rose from the dead, so shall they. He is but their Forerunner. He is the first fruits. Christ says to His church in Isaiah 26:19: "Thy dead men shall live, together with my dead body shall they arise." 1 Corinthians 15:22-23: "As in Adam all die, even so in Christ shall all be made alive, but everyone in his own order. Christ the first fruits; afterward they that are Christ's at His coming."

And then they shall also have communion with Christ in the glory of their bodies. Their bodies shall be made like Christ's glorious body (Philippians 3:21).

3. Lastly, there is a spiritual society between Christ and believers that is founded in their common partaking of benefits. And they are called to converse with Christ: they express their love and admiration of Him, and dependence upon Him and delight in Him, and their desires to Him with a sense of His presence in meditation, in prayer and in praises. They often look to Him, lifting up their hearts to Him.

And Christ is wont to meet with and mutually to communicate Himself to them. At such times, He will manifest Himself to them, and will by His Spirit make known His friendship and love, and teaches them and counsels and comforts them, as it were, by an inward spiritual work.

However, this many times is much interrupted in this world by darkness by reason of those remains of sin and corruption there are. But hereafter it will be perfect.

Application

USE 1. How great, then, is the privilege and happiness of believers, that they should be partakers with so great and glorious a Person in good things, that they should be partakers with Him in the rewards of His righteousness, that they should have communion with Him in His relation to the Father. How glorious a relation is that, to be the Son of God! And it is celebrated in Scripture. 1 John 3:1: "Behold, what manner of love the Father hath bestowed upon us."

How great to have communion with Him in partaking with Him in His Spirit, having His nature, His image, His own excellencies put upon us, and to be made partakers of His joy and comforts, and, above all, to be made partakers of His glory.

How wonderful is the grace of God to man, who is but a worm, that He should advance him to such dignity and blessedness, that they should be brought thus near to God. And how great a privilege is it to have society with Christ, to have Him for a Friend and a Companion; to meet with Him in our secret retirement; to have His gracious communication and the manifestations of Himself and His love, and of His accepting our love; to have Him coming to us, spiritually encouraging and comforting us, and confirming our hope in the promises, much more to enjoy His company forever in glory?

To have the favor of Christ in any measure would be a great privilege. To have any gift from so great a Person, as a token of His good will, would be a very great happiness. But to be partakers with Him, dear, intimate friends in His own Spirit, His own kingdom, His own happiness and His own glory, is a wonderful and unspeakable blessedness.

There is no blessing that Christ as Mediator partakes of but believers are in some way or other partakers of. All that He has, He gives to His people, as far as they can enjoy it. If these are the privileges of believers, well might it be said by Isaiah, when prophesying of gospel time, "Eye hath not seen, O God, beside Thee, what He hath prepared for him that waiteth for Him" (Isaiah 64:4).

USE 2. By the doctrine, we may learn a main thing wherein the blessedness consists of those who are redeemed by Christ. They have the advantage of the happiness of Adam in innocence. They are in Christ the Mediator, and so are partakers with Him of His blessedness.

Though Adam was in a state of friendship with God, and had communion with God by having His Spirit, His perfect image, and an uninterrupted conversation with God, yet he had not—nor never would have had—that communion with Christ the Mediator as believers have and are to have. Adam was not a partaker with Christ of His relation to the Father. He is called "the Son of God" (Luke 3:38). He was His son by creation, and in that he had God's image and was the object of God's fatherly love; yet he was not the son of God by being a member of His only begotten Son, and so was not a partaker of the Father's love to His Son and was not an heir with Him.

He would have been rewarded, if he had stood, for his own righteousness; but he never would have been a partaker of the reward of Christ's righteousness, that is so much more worthy and excellent. He would have had, if he had stood, great happiness and eternal life; but he

would not have been a partaker with Christ the Mediator
in His glory; he would not have been glorified together
with Him as a member, and partook of the same joy and
pleasure as a member partakes with the head. And as he
would not have had that near union with Christ, so neither
would he have had that intimate and familiar society with
Him as believers will have in heaven.

USE 3. By what has been said under this doctrine, we
learn that persons may be in great darkness and yet have
communion with Christ. They may be much in doubts
about their condition, and may have but little of the comforting presence of God, or of the manifestations of
Christ's love, and yet have communion with Christ.

'Tis that with which many afflict themselves. They are
in doubts about their condition and don't experience
much joy, and so they think that have no communion with
God or Christ, and so are ready to think that they don't
belong to God. But by what has been said we learn that
communion with Christ doesn't merely consist in those
comfortable manifestations of God's love and sweetness,
though that is a part; but it mainly consists in partaking of
Christ's Spirit, in being of His holy temper and disposition,
in partaking of His knowledge of the Father, partaking of
His love for God and His humility, meekness, and charity
to men. And therefore, if you have, upon examination,
found that you have these things, though but in a very imperfect degree, you may conclude that you have communion with Christ and be encouraged to seek more of that
other part of communion, which consists in partaking of
Christ's joy, and in a sweet, spiritual fearing and conversation with God. And to that end, put yourself in His way by

walking closely with Him, strictly treading in His path, and often thinking of Him and seeking Him in holy meditation, prayer and praise, and in His ordinances.

USE 4. Hence we learn what obligation Christians lie under to love one another, that all are thus united in one Head and have all communion with one Lord and all drink into one Spirit, and are all partakers together of the same happiness. In having communion with Christ, they have communion one with another (1 John 1:3, 6–7).

Christ prayed that His disciples might all have communion with Him for this end, that they might be united one to another. John 17:22: "And the glory which Thou gavest me have I given them; that they may be one, even as we are one."

USE OF EXHORTATION. First, to unbelievers, accept the calls of the gospel, seeing that if you so do, you will have communion with Christ. If you will but forsake sin and heartily give yourself up to Christ, He'll give Himself to you, and all that He has, the best that He Himself enjoys. You shall be a partaker with Him insofar as your nature is capable.

You aren't invited only to be a servant of Christ, but you are invited to be His friend. And you aren't only invited to be His friend, but to be His near, familiar, and intimate friend; to accept Christ's communication of His Spirit, of His divine knowledge, of His peace and His joy, of His glory, and also to accept His society and conversation.

Is not such an offer as this enough to move your heart and make you think of leaving all your sins, and to yield yourself to Christ Jesus and donate yourself to Him soul and body forever?

The second thing I would exhort you to is a serious and careful and joyful attendance on the Lord's Supper. It was instituted on purpose for Christians' communion with Christ and one another. There, in that ordinance, is represented how all the church of Christ together partakes with Christ in His spiritual benefits; how they partake with Him in the benefit of His suffering and righteousness, and partaking with Him of His Spirit and of His joy and comfort.

Therein also is represented Christ's friendship and society with His people as with His family at His table. It is there shown how they, in union and society, partake with Him of His blessedness, and there is sealed to them their communion with Him in glory. This bread and wine is given to believers as a pledge of their future glorious communion and partaking with Christ, when they shall drink new wine with Him in His kingdom.

And this is an ordinance that Christ delights to meet with His people in, and will give His blessing and his spiritual communion to the sincere, hearty, faithful attendants on it.

9

All Divine Blessings Are as Much in and through Christ as If They Were a Feast Provided of His Flesh That Was Given for Us

"And the bread which I give is My flesh, which I will give for the life of the world." John 6:51

(Preached June 1749)

In opening this text I would show:

1. The great benefit that we receive by Christ's life.

2. How this benefit is by Christ as natural life is by food.

3. The way in which this food is given us, that is, by the offering of Christ's human nature.

DOCTRINE. All divine blessings are as much in and through Christ as if they were a feast provided of His flesh that was given for us.

By divine blessings I intend all spiritual blessings, all the blessings the saints have in God.

PROPOSITION 1. All divine blessings to the fallen children of men are through Christ. We forfeited all blessings and wholly ruined ourselves. Christ has opened the fountain. All is through Christ, and through Him alone. Man

151

can do nothing by himself; nothing can be done by any mere creature. And therefore, through Him only can man find pardon, peace, safety, righteousness, a title to life, sanctification, every grace needed, victory over enemies, comfort, and fruitfulness.

These blessings are ours at death, in heaven, and at the resurrection, and they come to us through His purchase and intercession, through His Word and through His power.

PROPOSITION 2. All divine blessings are not only through Christ, but in Him we have comfort in our soul. John 1:4: "In Him was life." We have all divine blessings by having Christ. 1 John 5:11–12: "And this is the record, that God hath given to us eternal life, and this life is in His Son. He that hath the Son hath life; and he that hath not the Son of God hath not life." So we enjoy all by enjoying Christ. Colossians 2:10: "Ye are complete in Him."

We have all in the Person of Christ. All is in God, and God is enjoyed by the saints in the Person of Christ. All spiritual blessings in this world are in Christ.

The spiritual blessings of heaven are in Christ in two respects: (1) as He is the Fountain, He communicates of Himself, as it were, all inherent good; and (2) as His Person is their objective good and portion.

PROPOSITION 3. All divine blessings are in and through Christ by a union with Him. 2 Corinthians 13:5: "Christ is in you except ye be reprobates." Ephesians 3:17: "That Christ may dwell in your hearts." All divine blessings, except those that are relative, are by a personal union. And those are distinguished into relative and real. Relative blessings are more directly from the relative union; indeed this relative union is by a real union. A real union is the ground of it, but not properly a vital union. Real blessings are by the real and vital union with Christ.

PROPOSITION 4. All divine blessings are entirely through the giving of the flesh or human nature of Christ, for the Incarnation was the offering of the flesh to us. In this the Person of Christ has come nigh to us.

In and through Christ, human nature, Christ's beauty and excellence, are manifest, and especially in His sufferings. The infinite good that is in Him is this way exhibited on earth and in heaven. In this way love is manifested. The offering up of the flesh or human nature of Christ is the way in which all divine blessings are procured, and that in two respects: as an atonement and as a purchase.

Thus all divine blessings the saints receive, either in earth or heaven, are in and through Christ. Christ is their feast. His flesh and blood are their meat and drink (John 6:53–56). Spiritual blessings are often in Scripture compared to a great feast, as in Matthew 22 and Luke 14:15. Song of Solomon 5:1: "Eat, O friends." See also Isaiah 25:6, Proverbs 9, and Luke 15, the story of the prodigal son.

This feast has a vast variety of the richest dainties; here is a great fullness. But all this provision is, as it were, made out of Christ's flesh and blood.

The greatest feasts among the Jews were in their sacrifices: Passover, Pentecost, and the Feast of Tabernacles. Sometimes great feasts were held on particular occasions, such as bringing up the ark or the dedication of the Temple (1 Kings 8, the latter end).

So is the Christian feast the spiritual feast of the saints in this world. The eternal feast will be in heaven. This spiritual feast of the saints is represented in the Lord's Supper. Spiritual blessings in Scripture are often compared to those things that are eaten and drunk, such as manna. Christ's flesh is this manna.

The fruits of a tree are often compared to the Tree of Life. Song of Solomon 2:3 uses the apple tree. Wine is referred to in Song of Solomon 2:5: "Stay me with flagons." Zechariah 9:15: "Drink and make a noise." Scripture speaks of the water of life, of wine and milk. Christ's blood is this wine.

The saints do, as it were, continually live on a stream or river of divine goodness (Psalm 46). This stream is, as it were, Christ's blood. It has its fountain in Christ's wounds, in His wounded and broken heart. All divine blessings come flowing to the saints in this stream, and from it they receive all their worth, all their comforts, supports, and divine delight, all their glory.

The river of the water of life in heaven is the source of all their heavenly blessings. Hence their Fountain is that river of pleasures. Christ's own love and His Father's love flow to us in the stream of His blood. All the spiritual comforts and pleasure of the saints come to them through Christ's pain. All their riches come by His poverty. 2 Corinthians 8:9: "Being rich He made Himself poor." Their honor and glory come by His ignominy, His being brought forth in a stable, and having nowhere to lay His head. His hanging on the cross procured our sitting on a throne.

His countenance being disfigured and marred more than any procures this benefit to the saints, so that their faces shall shine as the sun. He was hated, despised, and rejected of men, being the object of cruelty, and subjected to the wrath of God. We are beloved of God because of the pouring forth of God's wrath into the soul of Christ. His wearing a crown of thorns was so that we might wear a crown of jewels.

PROPOSITION 5. All divine blessings are through believers receiving and, as it were, feeding on Christ as manifested and offered in the flesh, just as men receive and feed on their food to supply their emptiness and necessities.

Food is received with the natural appetite with relish; and there must be spiritual digestion in order to life, strength, and nourishment. Thus, a true coming to Christ is represented in Proverbs 9:5: "Come, eat of my bread and drink of the wine I have mixed."

Application

USE OF INFORMATION. Hence the greatness of those divine benefits, and why they are compared to a feast. Learn the excellency of the feast. The due consideration of the doctrine will teach us this in several ways:

1. The way in which this feast is provided. Infinite wisdom was displayed in providing it. Infinitely great and strange things were done to prepare it, many ages spent in preparing the way. That all divine blessings are through Christ, a Person so great and glorious, so infinitely dear to God, argues it to be greater than if it were done through our own righteousness.

In Christ is the long, continued, hard labor of a Person who is infinitely honorable. In Him is the price infinitely great, paid to purchase the provision.

2. The matter of the provision is the Son of God. John 6:55: "My flesh is meat indeed and My blood is drink indeed." This provision is angels' food, and much more is it ours. It is the Bread of God.

As with the sacrifices of old in these feasts the people partook with the priest and with God. So here the people partake with Christ and they partake with God. There is nothing in this sacrifice appropriated to God.

Christ ate and drank with His disciples at the first sacrament of the supper. And He speaks of drinking new wine with them in His heavenly Father's kingdom.

3. Another thing that shows the excellency of the spiritual benefit is that they are by enjoying Christ in such a manner, in a way of such a union.

USE OF REPROOF. Let this doctrine reprove those who despise those divine blessings.

USE OF EXHORTATION. Be exhorted to invite poor, miserable sinners to come and partake, to accept Christ's benefits. The doctrine leads to that which is the great condition, the great thing that you must be brought to in order to your salvation, to come and take Christ for your Foundation and live upon Him, and not upon the vanities of the world. He requires only that you forsake husks, forsake your filthiness that you have hitherto lived upon, and to come and eat. You are most freely invited.

This provision cost Christ infinitely dear, but it will cost you nothing; you are importunately invited. All persons concerned join together in inviting you. Your sins need to be no hindrance. Christ procured those benefits for such. He gave Himself for such.

In how friendly a manner you are invited. You are called to two things: (1) to forsake your husks and filthiness, and (2) to come to the feast and accept it as the food of your life.

Now, how reasonable and gracious are the terms. Christ seeks not His own good, but yours in it.

There will be a last call; you will hear no more invitations in hell. Now Christ stands at the door and knocks and says, "If you refuse, the time will come when you will come to My door and knock and cry, 'Lord, Lord.' "

(The manuscript ends here.)

Appendix

10

The Gospel Dispensation Is Finished Wholly and Entirely in Free and Glorious Grace

"And he shall bring forth the headstone thereof with shouting, crying, 'Grace, grace!' " Zechariah 4:7

The mercy of God is that attribute which we, the fallen, sinful race of Adam, stand in greatest need of; and God has been pleased, according to our needs, more gloriously to manifest this attribute than any other. The wonders of divine grace are the greatest of all wonders. The wonders of divine power and wisdom in making this great world are marvelous; other wonders of His justice in punishing sin are wonderful. Many wonderful things have happened since the creation of the world, but none like the wonders of grace. "Grace, grace!" is the sound that the gospel rings with. "Grace, grace!" will be that shout which will ring in heaven forever; and perhaps what the angels sang at the birth of Christ, of God's good will towards men, is the highest theme that ever they entered upon.

In order to understand the words of our text, take notice that the scope and design of the chapter is to comfort and encourage the children of Israel, returned out of their Babylonian captivity, in the building of Jerusalem and the temple. It seems that they were very much disheartened by reason of the opposition they met with in the work, and the want of the external glory of the former temple before the captivity, so that the priests and the Levites, and the chief of the fathers, wept aloud as the rest shouted at the sight, as you may see in Ezra 3:12: "But many of the priests and Levites, and chief of the fathers, who were ancient men, that had seen the first house, when the foundation of this house was laid before their eyes, wept with a loud voice, and many shouted aloud for joy." You may see a full account of their great oppositions and discouragements in the fourth and fifth chapters of Ezra.

The prophets Haggai and Zechariah were sent on this occasion to comfort them under those discouragements by foretelling the glories of the gospel that would be displayed in this latter house, which would render the glories of it far beyond the glories of the former, notwithstanding it was so far exceeded in what is external. Haggai 2:3-9: "Who is left among you that saw this house in her first glory? And how do ye see it now? Is it not in your eyes in comparison of it as nothing? Yet now be strong, O Zerubbabel, saith the Lord; and be strong, O Joshua, son of Josedech, the high priest; and be strong, all ye people of the land, saith the Lord, and work: for I am with you, saith the Lord of hosts, according to the word that I covenanted with you when ye came out of Egypt, so My Spirit remaineth among you. Fear ye not, for thus saith the Lord of hosts; Yet once, it is a little while, and I will shake the heavens, aye, and the earth, and the sea, and the dry land. And I will shake all nations, and the desire of all nations shall come; and I will fill this house with glory, saith the Lord of hosts. The silver is mine, and the gold is mine, saith the Lord of hosts. The glory of this latter house shall be greater than of the former, saith the Lord of hosts; and in this place will I give peace, saith the Lord of hosts."

See also, in the third chapter of this book, at the eighth verse: "Hear now, O Joshua the high priest, thou and thy fellows that sit before thee: for they are men wondered at; for behold, I will bring forth my servant, THE BRANCH." And the same subject is continued in this chapter, even the glorious grace of the gospel, which was to be manifested by Christ in this temple, particularly in our text: "And they shall bring forth the headstone with shouting, crying, 'Grace, grace' unto it." The headstone is that which entirely crowns and finishes the whole work, signifying that the entire gospel dispensation was to be finished in mere grace.

This stone was to be brought with repeated shouting or rejoicings at the grace of God, signifying the admirableness and gloriousness of this grace.

DOCTRINE: The gospel dispensation is finished wholly and entirely in free and glorious grace.

There is glorious grace shining in every part of the great work of redemption; the foundation is laid in grace, the superstructure is reared in grace, and the whole is finished in glorious grace.

If Adam had stood and persevered in obedience, he would have been made happy by mere bounty and goodness; for God was not obliged to reward Adam for his perfect obedience any otherwise than by covenant, for Adam by standing would not have merited happiness. But yet this grace would not have been such as the grace of the gospel, for he would have been saved upon the account of what he himself did; but the salvation of the gospel is given altogether freely. Romans 11:6: "And if by grace, then it is no more of works; otherwise grace is no more grace. But if it be of works, then it is no more grace; otherwise work is no more work."

That we may give you as full an explication of this doctrine as we can in a little space, we shall, first, show that free grace shines forth in the distinct parts of this wondrous work of redemption; second, we shall speak a little of the gloriousness of this grace.

1. But as to the first, every part of this work was performed of mere grace.

First, it was of free grace that God had any thoughts or designs of rescuing mankind after the fall. If there had not been an immense fountain of goodness in God, He would never have entertained any thoughts at all of ever redeeming us after our defection. Man was happy enough at first, and might have continued so to all eternity if he would; he was not compelled to fall. If he had not willfully and sinfully rebelled against God, he would never have been driven forth like an unworthy wretch, as he was. But although God had been so overflowing in His bounty to him as to make him head over the lower creation and ruler of all other creatures, and had planted a garden on purpose for his delight, and would have fixed him in an eternal happiness only on the reasonable condition of his obeying the easy commands of his Maker; but yet, notwithstanding all, he rebelled and turned over from God to the devil, out of a wicked ambition of being a god himself—not content in that happy state that he was in as man—and so rebelled against God's authority.

Now who but a God of boundless grace would not have been provoked after this to leave him as he was, in the miserable state into which he had brought himself by his disobedience, resolving to help him no more, leaving him to himself and to the punishment he had deserved, leaving him in the devil's hands where he had thrown himself, not being content in the arms of his Creator? Who but one of boundless grace would ever have entertained any thoughts of finding out a way for his recovery?

God had no manner of need of us or of our praises. He has enough in Himself for Himself, and neither needs nor desires any additions of happiness. And if He did need the worship of His creatures, He had thousands and ten thousands of angels; and if He had not enough, He could create more. Or He could have glorified His justice in man's eternal destruction and ruin, and could have with infinite ease created other beings, more perfect and glorious than man, eternally to sing His praises.

Second, but especially was it of rich and boundless grace that He gave His only Son for our restoration. By our fall we are cast down so low into sin and misery, so deeply plunged into a most miserable and sinful condition, that it may truly be said, although all things are infinitely easy to God with respect to His omnipotence, yet with respect to God's holiness and justice, God Himself could not redeem us without a great deal of cost, no, not without infinite costs; that is, not without the presence of that which is of infinite worth and value, even the blood of His

Son, and, in proper speaking, the blood of God, of a divine Person.

This was absolutely necessary in order to our redemption, because there was no other way of satisfying God's justice. When we were alienated, it must come to this: either we must die eternally or the Son of God must spill His blood; either we or God's own Son must suffer God's wrath, one of the two. Either miserable worms of the dust that had deserved it, or the glorious, amiable, beautiful, and innocent Son of God. The fall of man brought it to this; it must be determined one way or the other; and it was determined, by the strangely free and boundless grace of God, that His own Son should die so that the offending worms might be freed and set at liberty from their punishment, and that justice might make them happy. Here is grace indeed; well may we shout, "Grace, grace!" at this.

The heathens used to reckon that an only son slain in sacrifice was the greatest gift that could be offered to the gods. It was that which they used sometimes to offer in times of great distress; and in some parts of the world it is constantly at this day performed. But we have a stranger thing than that declared to us in the gospel; not that men sacrificed their only sons to God, but that God gave His only Son to be slain as a sacrifice for man. God once commanded Abraham to offer his only son to Him, and perhaps the faith and love of Abraham may be looked upon as wonderful, that he was willing to perform it (there are few who would do it in these days). But if you wonder at that, how wonderful is it that, instead of Abraham's offering his only son to God, God should give His only Son to be offered for Abraham, and for every child of Abraham. Certainly, you will acknowledge this to be a wonder not to be paralleled.

And besides, God did not do this for friends, but for enemies and haters of Him. He did not do it for loyal subjects, but for rebels. He did not do it for those who were His children, but for the children of the devil. He did not do it for those who were excellent, but for those who were more hateful than toads or vipers. He did not do it for those who could be in any way profitable or advantageous to Him, but for those who were so weak that, instead of profiting God, they were not able in the least to help themselves.

God has given fallen man such a gift that He has left nothing for man to do that he may be happy but only to receive what is given him. Though he has sinned, yet God requires no amends to be made by him. He requires of him no restoration; if they will receive His Son of Him, He requires neither money nor price. He is to do no penance in order to be forgiven. What God offers, He offers freely. God offers man eternal happiness upon far more gracious terms since he is fallen than before. Before, he was to do something himself for his happiness; he was to obey the law. But since he is fallen, God offers to save him for nothing, only if he will receive salvation as it is offered, that is, freely through Christ, by faith in Him.

Third, it was of mere grace that the Son was so freely willing to undertake our salvation. How cheerfully, yea, how joyfully, did He undertake it, although He Himself was the very person who was to suffer for man. Though He Himself was to bear man's sin and be made sin for him, yet how cheerfully He speaks in Psalm 40:7-8: "Lo, I come;

in the volume of the book it is written of Me, I delight to do Thy will, O God." He says in Proverbs 8:31 that His delights were with the sons of men, for so did He love them that it seems He Himself was willing to die in their place rather than that they should be miserable. He freely undertook this out of mere love and pity, for He never was and never will be repaid by them for His blood. 'Twas only that we might be happy.

Fourth, the application of the redemption of the gospel by the Holy Spirit is of mere grace. Although God the Father has provided a Savior for us, and Christ has come and died, and there is nothing wanting but our willing and hearty reception of Christ, yet we shall eternally perish yet if God is not gracious to us, and doesn't make application of Christ's benefits to our souls. We are dependent on free grace even for the ability to lay hold of Christ already offered, so entirely is the gospel dispensation of mere grace. Ephesians 2:8-10: "For by grace are you saved through faith, and that not of yourselves; it is the gift of God." That is, we shall be saved freely and for nothing if we will but accept Christ. But we are not able to do that of ourselves; it is the free gift of God, "not of works, lest any man should boast, for we are His workmanship, created in Christ Jesus unto good works, which God hath before ordained that we should walk in them."

2. We shall briefly speak to the gloriousness of this grace. As the grace of the gospel is altogether free, so it is glorious; the angels stoop down, with eyes full of wonder and joy, to look into it, and shout for gladness and admiration at the sight of it. How did the multitudes of heavenly hosts shout at the birth of Christ, crying, "Glory to God in

the highest; on earth peace and good will towards men!" Well may the topstone of this house be brought forth with shouting, crying, "Grace, grace!" to it.

All the attributes of God illustriously shine forth in the face of Jesus Christ. His wisdom in so contriving His power in conquering death and the devil, and the hard and rocky hearts of depraved men, and His justice in punishing the sins of men rather upon His own dear Son than let it go unpunished; but more especially in His grace, that sweet attribute, He has magnified His mercy above all His names.

The grace of God exhibited in the gospel is glorious, first, because of the greatness of it. Every circumstance of the gospel, grace surprisingly heightens it; let us look on what part we will, we shall see enough to fill us and all the angels in heaven with admiration forever. If we consider it as the grace of God the Father, and consider His greatness, His holiness, His power and justice, His immensity and eternity; if we diligently consider how great a being He is who took such pity and compassion on mankind, it is enough to astonish us. Or, if we consider ourselves, on whom this great God has bestowed this grace, we are nothing but worms, yea, less than worms, before God; and not only so, but sinful worms, worms swollen with enmity against God. If we consider Him by whom we receive grace, the Son of God who made heaven and, by His almighty power, is equal with the Father; if we consider the greatness of what He did, dying most ignominiously and painfully in our nature—it all infinitely heightens the grace of the gospel.

The grace of God exhibited in the gospel is glorious, second, because of the glorious fruit of it. No less than salvation and eternal glory are the fruits of this grace of the gospel; adoption, union with Christ, communion with God, the indwelling of the Holy Ghost, the heavenly happiness, the pleasure of the eternal paradise, the new Jerusalem, the glorious and triumphant resurrection of the body, and an everlasting reign with Christ in the height of glory, and pleasure and happiness—no less than these things are the effects of this marvelous grace.

What a vast difference is there between a poor, miserable sinner, full of sin, condemned to hellfire, and a saint shining forth in robes of glory, and crowned with a crown of victory and triumph; but no less difference than this is made in the same man by the grace of God in Christ.

Application

1. Hence we learn how they dishonor God and the gospel who depend on anything else but mere grace. The gospel is by far the most glorious manifestation of God's glory that ever was made to man, and the glory of the gospel is free grace and mere mercy. Now those who will not depend on this free grace do what they can to deprive the gospel of this glory, and sully the glory of God therein shining forth; they take away the praise, glory, and honor that is due to God by His free grace and mercy to men, and set up themselves as the objects of it, as if their salvation at least partly was owing to what they have done.

This must be very provoking and highly affronting to God; for miserable sinners, after they are fallen into such a miserable estate that it is impossible they should be saved by any other means than pure grace, and God is so gloriously rich in his goodness as to offer this free grace unto them out of pity to them, how provoking must it be to God for these miserable, helpless wretches to attribute any of their salvation to themselves!

It is not an opportunity to buy and procure our own salvation that God offers, but an opportunity to lay hold on that salvation that is already bought and procured for us. Neither are we able to do this of ourselves; it is the gift of God.

There are some who hope to be saved quite in another way than ever the gospel proposed, that is, by their own righteousness, by being so good and doing so well that God shall take their goodness as sufficient to counterbalance their sin that they have committed. And thereby they make their own goodness of equal value with Christ's blood. This conceit is very apt to creep into the proud heart of man.

Some openly profess to be able to merit salvation, as papists. Others hold that they are able to prepare and fit themselves for salvation already merited, or at least are able to do something towards it of themselves; and it is to be feared that many who don't openly profess either their own righteousness or their own strength do very much depend upon both. By this doctrine, how much they dishonor the free grace of the gospel!

2. Let all be exhorted to accept the grace of the gospel. One would think that there would be no need of such exhortations as this, but, alas, such is the dreadful wickedness and the horrible ingratitude of man's heart that he

needs an abundance of persuading and entreating to accept God's kindness when offered them. We would count it horrible ingratitude in a poor, necessitous creature to refuse our help and kindness when we, out of mere pity to him, offer to relieve and help him. If you should see a man in extremity of distress, and in a perishing necessity of help and relief, and you should lay out yourself with much labor and cost, out of compassion for him, that he might be relieved, how would you take it of him if he should proudly and spitefully refuse it and snuff at it instead of thanking you for it? Would you not look upon it as a very ungrateful, unreasonable, base thing? And why has not God a thousand times more cause to look upon you as base and ungrateful if you refuse His glorious grace in the gospel that He offers you? When God saw mankind in a most necessitous condition, in the greatest and extremist distress, being exposed to hellfire and eternal death, from which it was impossible he should ever deliver himself, or that ever he should be delivered by any other means, He took pity on them, and brought them from the jaws of destruction by His own blood. Now what great ingratitude is it for them to refuse such grace as this?

But so it is. Multitudes will not accept a free gift at the hands of the King of the World. They have the daring, horrible presumption to refuse a kindness offered by God Himself, and not to accept a gift at the hands of Jehovah, no, not His own Son, His own Son equal with Himself. Yea, they'll not accept Him though He dies for them; yea, though He dies a most tormenting death, though He dies that they may be delivered from hell, and that they may have heaven. They'll not accept this gift though they are in such necessity of it that they must be miserable forever without it. Yea, although God the Father invites and importunes them, they'll not accept it though the Son of God Himself knocks and calls at their door till His head is wet with the dew, and His locks with the drops of the night, arguing and pleading with them to accept Him for their own sakes, though He makes so many glorious promises, though He holds forth so many precious benefits to tempt them to happiness, perhaps for many years together, yet they obstinately refuse all. Was ever such ingratitude heard of, or can greater ingratitude be conceived of?

What would you have God do for you that you may accept it? Is the gift that He offers too small, that you think it too little for you to accept? Doesn't God offer you His Son, and what could He offer more? Yea, we may say that God Himself has no greater gift to offer. Did not the Son of God do enough for you that you won't accept Him? Did He not die, and what could He do more? Yea, we may say that the Son of God could not do a greater thing for man. Do you refuse because you want to be invited and wooed? You may hear Him from day to day, inviting you if you will but hearken. Or is it because you don't stand in need of God's grace? Don't you need it so much as that you must either receive it or be damned to all eternity, and what greater need can there possibly be?

Alas, miserable creatures that we are, instead of the gift of God offered in the gospel's not being great enough for us, we are not worthy of anything at all; we are less than the least of all God's mercies. Instead of deserving the dying Son of God, we are not worthy of the least crumb of bread, the least drop of water, or the least ray of light; instead of Christ's not having done enough for us by dying in such pain and ignominy, we are not worthy that He should so much as look on us instead of shedding his blood. We are not worthy that Christ should once make an offer of the least benefit instead of His so long urging us to be eternally happy.

Whoever continues to refuse Christ will find hereafter that, instead of his having no need of Him, the least drop of His blood would have been more worth to them than all the world; wherefore, let none be so ungrateful to God and so unwise for themselves as to refuse the glorious grace of the gospel.

3. Let those who have been made partakers of this free and glorious grace of God spend their lives much in praises and hallelujahs to God for the wonders of His mercy in their redemption. To you, O redeemed of the Lord, this doctrine most directly applies itself; you are those who have been made partakers of all this glorious grace of which you have now heard. 'Tis you that God entertained thoughts of restoring after your miserable fall into dreadful depravity and corruption, and into danger of the dreadful misery that unavoidably follows it; 'tis for you in particular that God gave His Son, yea, His only Son, and sent Him into the world; 'tis for you that the Son of God so freely gave Himself; 'tis for you that He was born, died, rose again and ascended, and intercedes; 'tis to you that there the free application of the fruit of these things is made. All this is done perfectly and altogether freely without any of your desert, without any of your righteousness or strength. Therefore, let your life be spent in praises

to God. When you praise Him in prayer, let it not be with coldness and indifference; when you praise Him in your closet, let your whole soul be active therein; when you praise Him in singing, don't barely make a noise, without any stirring of affection in the heart, without any internal melody. Surely, you have reason to shout, cry, "Grace, grace, be the topstone of the temple!" Certainly, you don't lack mercy and bounty to praise God; you only lack a heart and lively affections to praise Him with.

Surely, if the angels are so astonished at God's mercy to you, and do even shout with joy and admiration at the sight of God's grace to you, you yourself, on whom this grace is bestowed, have much more reason to shout.

Consider that the great part of your happiness in heaven, to all eternity, will consist in this: in praising of God for His free and glorious grace in redeeming you; and if you would spend more time about it on earth, you would find this world would be much more of a heaven to you than it is. Wherefore, do nothing while you are alive but speak and think and live God's praises.

11

The New Birth

"Except a man be born again he cannot see the
kingdom of God." John 3:3

(Preached March 1753)

In handling this text I shall, first, explain what is meant
by being born again and, second, show the necessity of it.

First, I shall explain how a man must be born again. A
man is not born again by baptism. Baptism is useless without the thing signified. God looks at the heart; what is external is useless without the circumcision of the heart
(Jeremiah 9:26), of the soul, as explained by Christ in verse
6, which plainly appears by verse 10. Baptism was not required until now.

But, affirmatively, hereby is meant that great change
that is wrought in man by the mighty power of God at his
conversion from sin to God, his being changed from a
wicked man to a holy one. And we shall show how that
man in this change is born again, whereby it will appear
what kind of change it is that is wrought.

By "birth" is meant the whole progress of the forma-
tion of man according to a course of nature.

1. In this change that is necessary in order to a man's
seeing the kingdom of God, he receives a new nature. In

man's first conception and birth he receives his nature. 'Tis by that he comes to be a human creature; 'tis by that he receives the essential parts of a man. The human soul is infused in the progress of this work of nature; hereby he receives the parts and shape of a human body with its senses and principles of action. 'Tis by this that men become more than senseless, inactive dust; 'tis by this that man receives life; that is, he receives both his sensitive and rational nature.

So, in the same manner, man, in that change whereby he becomes holy, receives a new nature. When a man is changed from a sinner to a saint, the change is not a mere change of manners, or a change in outward appearance, but 'tis a change of nature. In this change a man receives a nature that is entirely diverse from the nature he had before, or anything that he had in that nature. 'Tis as truly and entirely different as the nature of man is from the the nature of mere clay or earth.

The change that is wrought is not such a change as may be wrought by education. A child may be mightily altered in many things by instruction, government, and example. There is a vast alteration in the outward behavior, and in many qualifications of the child; but there is no proper change of nature. 'Tis not such a change as may be brought about by custom. Men may contract habits; they may have many old habits eradicated and new ones inrooted, but there may be no proper change of nature, as there is in conversion. The change of man from a sinner to a saint is not a moral change but a physical one. A moral change is wrought by human instruction, government, and example, and by a man in himself by resolution and pains. But these changes don't reach to the nature of the soul so as to change it.

The nature of man consists in principles of perception and principles of action; the human nature whereby man differs from a beast or a tree consists in principles. Men's faculties are principles; the natural appetites are principles; the love of pleasures and the aversion to pain, the love of honor, are principles.

But when man is changed from a sinner to a saint, he has new principles of perception and action, principles that are entirely diverse, and not merely arising from a new disposition of the old, as contracted habits and those changes that are wrought by education do. They are principles that are vastly superior to those he had before, superior to 'em in such a manner that it would be as impossible that they should arise from them as it is that a principle of reason should arise from a power of sensation, and so that a brute could be changed into a rational creature without a physical change.

There is infused in conversion a principle of spiritual understanding and spiritual action that is as far above any principles that man had before as the heaven is high above the earth. And this change of nature is such that a man not only acts above what he did before, but contrary to what he did before. The principles that were before, as they were ungoverned and inordinate, were most contrary to those supernatural principles that are infused; they are sinful, and these are mortified when spiritual principles are infused.

2. The change is universal, of the whole man. Man, in his first birth or conception, receives the beginnings of all

that belongs to the human nature; all that is both soul and body are then begun; all the faculties of the soul are then received, and all the members of the body, every vein and sinew, and all the senses. So when a man is changed from a sinner to a saint, the whole man is renewed or made new. Ephesians 4:22–24: "That ye put off concerning the former conversation the old man, which is corrupt according to the deceitful lusts, and that ye put on the new man, which after God is created in righteousness and true holiness."

The whole man is sanctified. 1 Thessalonians 5:23: "And the very God of peace sanctify you wholly, and I pray God your whole spirit and soul and body be preserved blameless." So in conversion there is a new principle of understanding, a principle whereby the soul knows God and understands His glory and excellency, and the truth and excellency of spiritual things, the great things of God's Word, the glorious doctrines of the gospel and things pertaining to Christ the Savior which the soul had no power to understand before. It is as if there were added to the soul eyes to see that before was blind and had no eyes (Deuteronomy 29:4).

There is a new principle of will and inclination. The man now loves God and loves Christ, whom he could not love before he relishes holiness; he now loves holy and heavenly things, which he could not relish before. He could not find these things in his heart before, so that 'tis as if God gave man a new heart. Ezekiel 36:26: "A new heart will I give unto you, and a new spirit will I put within you."

The body also, in a new sense, the whole spirit, soul, and body, is renewed and sanctified. The members of the body are as new as the purposes they are subservient to.

3. In that change whereby a man is changed from a sinner to a saint, man does, as it were, receive being. When men are conceived and born they receive their beings; so also in this change there is that which is equivalent to a man's receiving being. Man, by the fall and corruption of his nature, is ruined, and is reduced to a state in many respects lower than when he was in his first dust. He was so spoiled and ruined that it was equivalent to a thing being lost that rendered his being either excellent or happy, so that he might as well not be; yea, he was brought to a state worse than his first nothing. Not only has he lost all that was good, but, being plunged into all evil, both of sin and misery, he is spiritually dead and is condemned to eternal death.

Therefore, when a man is converted, he does, as it were, receive his being again; and therefore this change is called a creation as well as a new birth. Ephesians 2:10: "For we are His workmanship, created in Christ Jesus."

4. They come into a new existence. 2 Corinthians 5:17 says that old things are done away with while all things are become new.

5. This change is as a birth because it is brought to pass by stated means. It is the same as a birth rather than an immediate creation. 'Tis God who makes man new as truly as He made our first parents. But now it is in a certain stated way, and according to a fixed law of nature. God could, if He pleased, convert men immediately without the use of any means at all, but He does not do so. But there are stated means that are appointed and fixed by the law of grace that are constantly made use of in producing this

effect. Conversion is wrought by the Word and by ordinances. There is an ordinary way of the Spirit's working, and we call this His preparatory work.

6. At the new birth a man is born into a state like that of children (Matthew 18:3), into an imperfect state, a growing state. 1 Peter 1:24: "All flesh is as grass, and all the glory of man as the flower of the grass. The grass withereth and the flower thereof falleth away." And 1 Peter 2:2: "As newborn babes, desire the sincere milk of the Word, that ye may grow thereby."

We are often called "little children" by Christ. John 13:33: "Little children, yet a little while I am with you." And by the apostles Paul and John. Galatians 4:19: "My little children, of whom I travail in birth till Christ be formed in you." See also 1 John 2 and other places.

7. Hereby we become members of a family. Ephesians 2:19 speaks of the household of God. Ephesians 3:15 speaks of the whole family in heaven and earth. Believers have new relations. God is their Father and Christ is their elder brother. The saints are Christ's brethren (Hebrews 2:11–12). Matthew 23:8: "But be not ye called Rabbi; for one is your Master, even Christ, and all ye are brethren."

Second, I come now to give some reasons for the need of the new birth.

REASON 1. The end of man's being is not reached in the first birth. Man by his first birth receives being; what is attained is that he should have an existence in this world. But he doesn't attain the end of his being, and therefore there is need that he should be born again. By the first birth he is made, but the end for which he is made is not reached.

He comes into the world with those defects, with a want of those essential things that are as necessary in order to obtaining the end of his being as his being itself. And his being without these things will as wholly and entirely frustrate the design of his being as if he wanted being itself. 'Tis not merely necessary that man should be in order to his obtaining the end of his being, but he must be with such and such principles and qualifications which, if he wants, he will as certainly and entirely fail to reach his end as if he remained nothing as at first. To have a being is one step towards man's obtaining the end of his being; but if no other step is taken, he as entirely fails to reach his end as if none was taken. It being thus that man in his first birth is born with those defects, there is a necessity of a new birth because a man had as well not be as not obtain the end of his being.

But here, in order to the right understanding of what we mean when we say that the end of a man's being is not reached in his first birth, and that there is a necessity of a new birth in order the end of his existence being obtained, it is not to be taken as though God were properly frustrated in His giving any man a being, whether he is born again or not. But when we speak of the end of man's being, it may be taken in two ways. It may be taken either for that universal end that man has in common with all other things, which is God's glory. This end, which is the most ultimate, must and shall be obtained whatsoever the defects of man's nature are. Whether a man is born again or not, God will so order and overrule things that this end shall be obtained. God takes this for His own care, the obtaining of this end. He doesn't trust this to any creature.

Then, by the end of man in another sense is to be understood that particular good that is the design of man's particular nature, which the human nature is capable of and adopted to particularly, which may be said to be the genuine design of this particular piece of workmanship. There is a particular use that the nature of man seems evidently to be designed and capacitated, which may be said to be the proper use of the powers of the human nature; thus the proper use of the human understanding is to know God, and the proper use of the human will and affections is to love God and enjoy Him. That use which is the genuine design of human nature and powers may be said to be the proper end of man, as the proper end of a house is to dwell in and the proper end of a garment to clothe man with and the proper end of a vessel is to contain. 'Tis this proper end of man that man, in his first birth, fails of, and, as if a potter makes a vessel that is broken and leaky, the proper end of a vessel is not obtained. If a man plants a fruit tree and it bears no fruit, the proper end is not obtained; however, it may have another use, which is to burn (Matthew 7:19).

The proper end of man is to glorify God in a way of knowing, loving, praising, and serving Him. But this end is not reached in the first birth because the vessel is broken. Man is born with essential defects; it is needful that man, in order to obtain his proper end, should not only have natural principles, or those principles that belong and are essential to the human nature, but supernatural principles, those principles that are superior to the natural and were given to govern the natural, and which the natural principles were given to be subordinate to. The principles of spiritual life, of spiritual understanding, inclination, and action, these principles are absolutely necessary in man in order to his serving and glorifying God. But man in his first birth is born without them, and the natural inferior principles can do nothing but evil without them. Therefore, there is need of a new birth in order to his being received and accepted by God and admitted into His kingdom; for 'tis not reasonable to suppose that those will be admitted and accepted as God's people in His kingdom, and as His children in His family, who don't answer the end of their beings. When a vessel is marred in the making, so that it won't answer the end of a vessel, there is need of its being made over again by the potter. Jeremiah 18:3–4: "Then I went down to the potter's house, and behold he wrought a work on the wheels; and the vessel that he made of clay was marred in the hand of the potter. So he made it again another vessel."

REASON 2. Man's proper excellency and perfection is not attained in the first birth. By the first birth man becomes man, but does not have those principles and endowments that are the excellency and glory of manhood. The true excellency of man consists in the image of God; but man by the fall lost this image of God. He has lost the divine nature, so that the nature of man is lost; it is a spoiled, ruined thing, and we all, as we come into the world, come with this defect of the image of God and are thus ruined. Therefore we stand in need of another birth so that we may attain our proper perfection. God made man at first very good. Genesis 1:31: "God saw everything that He had made, and behold, it was very good." But this piece of God's workmanship, that is, man, as he now comes into the world in his first birth, is not so. But, on the contrary, he is very bad, and therefore men need to be born again in order to their being owned and blessed by God as His people.

REASON 3. Man by the first birth does not attain to a capacity of enjoying his proper happiness, and therefore 'tis necessary that he should be born again. Indeed, every man is capable of enjoying happiness remotely, that is, he is capable without the addition of any new faculties of receiving those principles whereby he shall be prepared and immediately capacitated for the enjoyment of his proper happiness. He is capable of obtaining to true happiness without the addition of any new faculties, but not without the addition of new principles.

Man's proper happiness consists in the enjoyment of God. But it is not possible that man should enjoy God with only those things in him that he receives by the first birth. So there is this necessity of man's being born again in order to his obtaining the kingdom of God; it is not possible in nature that he should see the kingdom of God with only those principles of nature that he receives by his first birth. So man still remains nothing, or as bad as nothing.

REASON 4. It is necessary that man should be born again because those things that are wanting can't be attained by any modification whatsoever of anything that man receives by his first birth. These natural principles that man has by his first birth, let them be turned and disposed and modified how they will, we never can attain by that means to those supernatural principles that are wanting which are necessary in order to man's obtaining his proper end, and his true excellency, and in order to his

being in a capacity to enjoy true happiness, the happiness
of the kingdom of God.

Man by his first birth has natural faculties of understanding and will; he has self-love; he has a love for happiness and an aversion to misery. And these principles may
be so modified and directed that man may thereby attain
to great learning and human knowledge, and may excel in
outward virtue and have a love for it. But man by this
means can never come to the true knowledge of the glory
of God and the excellency of Christ; nor can he come to a
sincere and unfeigned love for God, or have a spiritual
appetite, or be in a capacity for the reception of spiritual
enjoyments.

If any modifying of any principles that man has by his
first birth could cause to arise those other principles that
are wanting, there would be no need of their being new
men; the nature of man might be mended without a new
birth. If true love for God could by any means be made to
arise from any modifications of self-love, a man would not
need to be newborn in order to his loving God. But it is
not so.

Application

1. If there is so great a change to be wrought, how unreasonable is the security of multitudes of men. Every man
who shall not see the kingdom of heaven will feel the torments of hell to all eternity, so that, as except he is born
again, he cannot see the kingdom of God, so he cannot
escape the damnation of hell. This is a rule that has no exceptions; 'tis fixed and unalterable, as is intimated by the

manner of expression in the text, "Verily, verily." And yet what a multitude of men are there who have experienced no such change, who are most remote from it, who are yet careless and secure. They take little thought; they aren't inquiring and contriving what they shall do that they may be born again, nor are they concerning themselves about it. They seem to live easy and undisturbed. Yea, and many of those who have been well instructed in this doctrine of the necessity of being born again aren't seeking such a change, nor doing anything towards it, but let time pass without taking any thought as to how it passes, how fast it slips away, and how soon it will all be gone and their glass will be run and their one opportunity slipped. They don't know how soon it will be, but they don't trouble themselves about it. They have something else to mind; they mind the world and are concerned how to increase their estates, or mind their pleasures and their company, and they let this matter of their being born again be as it will.

They are careless and secure, though there is no appearance of any such change, nor anything done towards it. 'Tis a very remote thing; there appears nothing in them that tends that way; there appears nothing in them that gives any reasonable prospect of any such a thing that renders it probable that it ever will be. There is no probability of it, and yet they are very secure, and their minds are very much taken up with other things. How little likelihood is there that even so great a change as being born again will ever be obtained without striving and taking considerable pains; but yet they take no pains. They don't strive for it; yea, many of them don't think of striving for it, and yet aren't terrified with the thought that except they are born again before they die they must certainly be damned forever. Yea, not only do they do nothing towards such a change, but they are continually setting themselves at a greater and greater distance from it. They are, as fast as they can, laying blocks in the way, making it more and more unlikely that they shall ever be the subjects of such a change. So there is no likelihood of their being converted, and yet they are not concerned about it. How wonderfully unreasonable is the security of those sinners who know the Bible and hear such doctrines preached out of it.

2. Hence the great mistake of those who flatter themselves that they are converted, who never experienced any remarkable, habitual change in their hearts. Being born again is surely a great and remarkable thing, as we have described it. It certainly appears to be so. How unreasonable then is the mistake of those who, when they look back, can't return in their thoughts to any remarkable change that ever they experienced, and who aren't now in any way remarkably different in their hearts, tempers, and dispositions from what they always have been, or from what they were before their supposed conversion; who are in no way remarkably new in their sense and disposition about spiritual and heavenly things; who never differ from what they used to be in their thoughts and sense about God and Jesus Christ, about the gospel and way of salvation, about this world and the future; who are as worldly as ever, and whose change is not lasting; who have only superficial, transient affections, whose change is chiefly outward—not in the principles and nature, but in the outward manners and customs.

There are many who think themselves to be born

again, who think that they have been the subjects of this change that is so great, so universal, as it were, a coming out of nothing into being, who never have experienced any change of nature at all. These persons haven't had one new principle added nor one sinful disposition really mortified; they never saw one example of divine light, never saw the least of God's or Christ's glory, nor have ever put forth one act of love for God in their lives. They think themselves now made and renewed in the whole man who never have had one finger renewed, if I may use such an expression.

USE OF EXAMINATION. Examine whether or not you are new born. Examine whether or not you are as little children, humble (Matthew 18:3). Examine whether or not, as newborn babes, you desire the sincere milk, whether or not you are governed by spiritual appetites (see 1 Peter 2:2). Examine whether you are a follower of God as a dear child, and whether you walk as a child of the light and of the day. Examine whether you follow God as children with a filial disposition, with love, with reverence, with dependence as a little child on a father, imitating Him, obeying Him in everything (Ephesians 5:1).

USE OF DIRECTION. Be in the steady and diligent use of appointed means. Earnestly seek it of God, who is the Father. Use the Word, which is as the seed. 1 Corinthians 4:15: "I have begotten you through the gospel." Use the law, which causes the pangs of the new birth. Use the ordinances administered in the church, which is our mother; believers are the children of the church. See Isaiah 49:20–21 and Isaiah 54:1. Galatians 4:26: "But Jerusalem which is above, which is the mother of us all."

Be speedy; don't halt; don't wait for better times. Be earnest; don't spend time contriving to snare yourself. Take heed that you aren't undone through the deceitfulness of sin. Avoid temptation; don't strive only in some duties. And don't flatter yourself that you are more likely to be saved than other sinners.

12

When God Sends His Messengers to Preach His Word, His Word Shall Not Be in Vain

"But when I speak with thee, I will open thy mouth, and thou shalt say unto them, 'Thus saith the Lord God, "He that heareth, let him hear; and he that forbeareth, let him forbear " '; for they are a rebellious house." Ezekiel 3:27

Ezekiel was a prophet that God raised up in Chaldea amongst the captives there who were carried away with King Jehoiachim, to warn the people of the Jews who were yet in Judea under King Zedekiah of the approaching destruction that God would bring upon them if they did not turn from their evil ways.

The Jews at that time were so obstinate that, although God had for a long time been warning them by His prophets, one and another of them, and particularly by the prophet Jeremiah, who prophesied many years before and continued in the time of the captivity, and though God had actually begun to fulfill His word by His prophets in Jehoiachim's captivity [1:2], wherein were carried away all the principal men of the land, and only the poor and baser sort were left, yet those who remained hardened their necks and refused to hear God's Word by His prophets. They stubbornly continued in their wickedness.

God nevertheless, besides the prophet Jeremiah, sends Ezekiel to them, and tells him how obstinate and rebellious a people He sent him to, how unlikely to hearken to Him, as in chapter 2:3–4 of the context. He forewarns him that going and preaching the Word of God to them would be like going amongst briars and thorns and scorpions. They would show themselves so perverse, so proud and spiteful (2:6).

Yea, He tells him plainly in 3:7 that they would not hearken to him: "But the house of Israel will not hearken unto thee; for the house of Israel are impudent and hard-hearted." But yet He bids him go and speak to them whether they would hear or whether they would forbear. Here we have an account in the context of God's fore-warning Ezekiel of his being hindered for a while from speaking His words, and of God's afterwards opening his mouth again (3:25–27).

And now, beforehand, God gives him this message to deliver to 'em when his mouth shall be opened again, to introduce the word that God should then send him with. He bids him say unto them, "Thus saith the Lord God, 'He that heareth, let him hear; and he that forbeareth, let him forbear'; for they are a rebellious house" (3:27).

They, in their stubborn and proud opposition to God's prophets, and to the Word of God in their mouths, were not sensible that they hurt none but themselves by it. They seemed maliciously to oppose themselves to God and His prophets, as though they imagined that they were princi-pally concerned in the word that was delivered, and as though God was an enemy within their reach. They were not sensible how, by opposing Him, they were their own worst enemies.

These two propositions seem to be implied in the words.

DOCTRINE: When God sends His messengers to preach His Word, His Word shall not be in vain; or, **God shall not be frustrated whether men hear or whether they forbear.**

God won't be frustrated in sending them. He will obtain His end, let men treat His Word how they will. If they cast it by, if they treat it with contempt and show never so little regard for it, yet God will take care and see that He doesn't miss His end. He will see that His Word does its work some way or another.

Though men may be regardless of His Word, yet God is not, nor will He be regardless of it. Though they are in no way careful whether God's end is obtained or not, yet God Himself will be careful of it. His Word shall not be neglected by Him.

God Himself has declared that His Word shall not return to Him void. Isaiah 55:10: "For as the rain cometh down, and the snow from heaven, and returneth not thither, but watereth the earth, and maketh it bring forth [and] bud, that it may give seed to the sower, and bread to the eater, so shall My Word be that goeth out of My mouth; it shall not return unto Me void, but it shall accomplish that which I please, and it shall prosper in the thing whereto I sent it." Here note:

1. There are many men who refuse to hear God's Word with which God sends His messengers to them.

First, let 'em hear never so many calls and gospel invitations, they refuse to come to Christ and accept Him as a
Savior. 'Tis a thing that many will not be really convinced
of, that there is a Savior, that Jesus Christ is the Son of God
and the Savior of the world. However light is set before
them, yet their hearts are so opposed to the light that they
will not receive it. They "love darkness rather than light
because their hearts and deeds are evil" (John 3:19).

And men's wills are opposed to the gospel. The gospel,
the Savior, and His way of salvation don't suit their natural
inclinations. The way of salvation is too holy for 'em; it ascribes too much to God and not enough to themselves.
They can see no beauty in Christ wherefore they should
desire Him; and it is impossible they should be persuaded
to love Christ if they see no beauty in Him. They see no
excellence, no fitness in the way of salvation; but, on the
contrary, 'tis a way contrary to the strongest bent and inclination of their souls.

They have many things in their hearts that keep 'em
from closing with Jesus Christ. There is their worldly-
mindedness. When God's messengers are sent forth to call
them, they begin to make excuses. One has bought a piece
of land, and another has bought cattle and his heart is
upon them, and another has married a wife and therefore
cannot come (Luke 14:18–20). And so they go away, one
to his farm and another to his merchandise.

There are many who will not be persuaded to come off
from their own righteousness. They have gotten into a way
of trusting themselves and their own works, and so don't
see their need of Christ. They will neither be persuaded to
trust in Christ as their high priest to make satisfaction for

'em and recommendation to God by His righteousness, nor will they receive Christ's rule and government over 'em.

And telling men of their perishing necessity of a Savior, their guilt, and setting forth the sufficiency of Christ's salvation; telling them what a complete redemption Christ has wrought and how fully His blood has satisfied divine justice, how acceptable Christ's obedience is to God, how safe it is appearing in His righteousness, how glorious the blessings are that He has purchased, how amiable this person of Jesus Christ is, and how willing He is, how He has invited 'em to Him—it all signifies nothing to persuade them. There is such an opposition to their natures to Christ and the gospel that they will not come to Him.

Thus it was with the Jews of old. They had abundant means used with them to persuade them to come to Christ. John the Baptist had borne witness of Him, and God the Father had borne witness to Him by a voice from heaven. His works, His many miracles, had been witness of Him; and the Scriptures of the Old Testament abundantly bore witness of Him. And yet they rejected Him; they obstinately refused to receive Him as a Savior. John 5:40: "And ye will not come to Me that ye might have life."

Second, there are many who will not be persuaded by God's Word to seek their salvation and to be concerned for the general welfare of their precious and immortal souls, let the messengers of God use what arguments they will from the Word of God.

If they tell 'em of hell and set forth to 'em the terribleness of its torments, and how dreadful a thing it is to suffer for all eternity without any hope of ever being delivered, how unable they will be to bear the wrath of an Almighty Being; if they are told how uncertain they are of their lives, how uncertain the continuance of their opportunity to obtain salvation is, what a risk they run in delaying and putting off, how common it is for persons who do so to be surprised with death and driven away in their wickedness, hurried out of the world in an unprepared condition, how common it is for men to lament their sloth and neglect of their souls upon a death bed, what danger there is of God's giving 'em up to hardness of heart, and the like—yet it doesn't move 'em. They are as stupid and senseless as stones.

They come to meetings from one Sabbath to another and hear God's Word, but all that can be said to 'em won't awaken 'em; it won't persuade 'em to take pains that they may be saved.

How many men are there who aren't persuaded, and won't be persuaded, so much as to pray in any constant way that they may be saved. Yea, they are so careless about the salvation of their souls that they seldom think of it with any seriousness or concern of mind.

Third, there are many who won't be persuaded by anything that can be said to 'em by the Word of God to forsake their vices and ways of known sin. They live in a way of gratifying some lust or other, and they know it to be a sin. They can't but have light enough to know it, and they will not forsake it.

If they are told of God's command, and have the heinousness of that particular sin set before 'em, and are told how dreadfully provoking it is to God to obstinately go on in known wickedness against warnings, how great the danger is that God will be provoked to swear in His wrath that they shall never enter into His rest, yet they are bold to go on still. They'll go right from hearing the Word to their old way of wickedness again; the Word of God that they hear doesn't alter 'em at all.

Thus did the children of Israel before and in the time of the captivity: they would not forsake their idolatries and their other wickedness for all that the prophets said to 'em. And when that remnant that fled into Egypt was warned by the prophet Jeremiah, they said to Jeremiah, "As to the word that thou hast spoken unto us in the name of the Lord, we will not hearken unto thee. But we will certainly do whatsoever thing goeth forth out of our own mouth, to burn incense to the queen of heaven, and to pour out the drink offerings unto her, as we have done, we, and our fathers, our kings, and our princes in the cities of Judah, and in the streets of Jerusalem; for then had we plenty of victuals, and were well, and saw no evil" (Jeremiah 44:16–17). There are many who practically say after the same manner as those Jews did.

Fourth, there are many who take so little notice of God's Word by His messengers that 'tis not their aim to consider or lay up what is said. They come to meetings, but it is only in conformity to custom. 'Tis not what they aim at by coming to meetings that they may hear anything in order to their own practice and for their own souls' good. For they, when they come, take no sort of pains to attend to and to apply it to themselves. They hear the words, it may be, but it is without any reflection about 'em. They don't endeavor to remember 'em. They sit and hear as if what they heard was what did in no way concern them. So do they treat the message of the Most High God to 'em.

Fifth, there are some who take so little notice of the message that is delivered to 'em from God that they don't so much as hear it so as to know what is spoken. Their thoughts are intent upon something else; their hearts are in the ends of the earth. They are gazing about the assembly minding this and the other person that is in it, or they are thinking of their worldly business. They are contriving how to do this or that piece of work and accomplish such and such a design, or they are thinking of this or that other occurrence that has lately passed, or of some business or diversion they have lately been engaged in, or they are feeding their lusts in their imaginations, so that they don't know what it is that the minister says. And it may be they are whispering with their companions or with them who sit next to them, or they are asleep and are dreaming instead of hearing the Word of God.

2. However men disregard His Word, yet God will not be frustrated. He will see to it that His Word shall not be in vain or without effect. God will make His Word to obtain His ends in one way or the other. If it isn't effectual upon men with respect to that which is the direct design of it, which is convincing, reforming, and converting men, yet God will make it to take effect another way whereby He will glorify Himself.

God's end in His Word, as in His works, is to glorify Himself. He had this end in indicting the Scriptures, and He has this end in sending forth His messengers. And there is no doubt but God will see to it that that end is obtained, that His Word shall be the occasion of glory to His name.

Here, first, we will show what effect the Word will have upon such persons, or rather what it will be an occasion of in them as will not hear; and, second, how that effect will be to the glory of God.

The effects that the Word of God will have upon such persons as won't hear it, or what the Word will be an occasion of in 'em, will be twofold: there are effects in this world and in another.

The effects in this world are these: The Word of God will exceedingly enhance their guilt. It will enhance their guilt in these two ways: both as they will have their obstinacy and rebellion of theirs to answer for, and their refusing to hear the Word of God. They "add rebellion to their sin," as it is expressed in Job 34:37. This wickedness of refusing to hear warnings and counsels and gracious offers after their other wickedness shows the dreadful perverseness of their hearts, and terribly provokes the wrath of God.

And then also the sins that they commit afterwards are exceedingly aggravated thereby. When they go on in sin after they have been so instructed and warned, their sin is looked upon by God as much more heinous and contracts much more guilt. Thus, if a person neglects prayer or is intemperate or unclean after he has been warned from the Word of God and in His name against it, his sin is the more exceedingly sinful for it.

Another thing the Word of God is the occasion of in this world in such persons is that it hardens their hearts to hear the Word of God and the calls and warnings and threatenings of it; and to refuse them exceedingly establishes the power and dominion of sin in the heart, as a king's dominion is the more established by overcoming his enemies.

After men have been used to hear the Word of God and to condemn it, it is a harder thing to convince 'em or to in any way affect 'em with that which is good; sin and wickedness is sealed by it. What a message was Isaiah sent with to the people of Israel. Isaiah 6:9–10: "Go, and tell this people, 'Hear indeed, but understand not; see ye indeed, but perceive not.' Make the heart of this people fat, and make their ears heavy; lest they should see with their eyes, and hear with their ears, and understand with their heart, and be converted, and be healed."

As to the effects it will have upon 'em in another world:

(1) Their punishment will be the more dreadful. Thus we learn that those who have had the Word of God preached to 'em, and have refused to hearken to it, they have the most dreadful punishment in another world. What does Christ say of Bethsaida? "Woe unto thee, Bethsaida! For if the mighty works which were done in you had been done in Tyre and Sidon, they would have repented long ago in sackcloth and ashes" (Matthew 11:21). And God tells the children of Israel in Amos 3:2, "You only have I known of all the families of the earth; therefore will I punish you for all your iniquities." They doubtless will have the heavier punishment if their guilt is enhanced and their hearts hardened, as we have shown.

Thus the Word of God, as it will be a savor of life to some, so in others it will be a savor of death. 2 Corinthians

2:15–16: "For we are unto God a sweet savor of Christ in them that are saved and in them that perish: to the one we are a savor of death unto death; to the other we are a savor of life unto life."

As it is of the personal, so it is of the revealed Word of God. It is to some a stone of stumbling and rock of offense. Christ says, "For judgment I am come into the world, that they which see not might see; and that they which see might be made blind" (John 9:39).

(2) Those who thus refuse to hear the Word that is preached to 'em in this world will regard it in another world. Now the Word of God doesn't take any hold of 'em; it doesn't affect 'em. But then it will take hold of 'em. It will work up in 'em then, however it has been slighted by 'em now. Now they don't take the pains to consider it or reflect upon it, but then they will not be able to help reflecting on it. This is intimated in these words: "And whether they hear, or whether they will forbear, yet shall know that there has been a prophet among them" (Ezekiel 2:5). When the words of the prophet come to be fulfilled, then they shall consider what has been said to 'em, as in Ezekiel 33:33: "And when this cometh to pass (lo, it will come), then shall they know that there has been a prophet among 'em."

When wicked men come to be in hell, then they will believe that what God's messengers said to 'em was true, or rather they will know it to be so. When they were told what a dreadful punishment God threatened, it did not seem to 'em a reality. They took little notice of it. But now it will be brought to their minds how they were warned and what counsels they had been given, what offers and invitations were made them. And now they will be of another mind about them. They'll regard them now. They'll be sensible now of how great importance they were, when it will be too late to any other purpose to sharpen and envenom the sting of their consciences and augment their misery.

Second, God will have His glory by these effects:

1. Hereby God will to a greater degree glorify the terribleness of His wrath. One design He has upon His heart is to glorify His wrath. God is willing to show His wrath and make the power of it known (Romans 9:22). The Word of God, when it is not regarded by men, is an occasion of filling up the measure of their sin, and so of filling up the measure of their punishments. When it does men no good, it ripens the grapes for the wine press, and fits them for fuel for hellfire.

2. It renders justice in their damnation the more conspicuous. And so God glorifies His justice the more in their destruction, for their guilt becomes greater and more notorious and they become more inexcusable; and their own consciences will condemn them the more and will justify the Judge in the sentence He passes upon them. The iniquity of such men cries aloud for vengeance, and the justice of God in the destruction of such men as have refused His Word will be especially clear and evident in the sight of men and angels.

Thus God is not frustrated. His Word doesn't return to Him void. There are two reasons for this:

REASON 1. God is infinitely wise and powerful, and is able to obtain His end whether men will hear or whether men will forbear.

REASON 2. The Word of God is too honorable and precious to be suffered to be in vain. 'Tis fitting that the Word of so great a God should take effect, should accomplish that. 'Tis the honor of the Word that, though men don't honor it, God will.

Application

USE OF ENCOURAGEMENT. Ministers should not neglect faithfully to preach the Word of God, however regardless men are of their message.

'Tis a discouraging thing. Ministers are to aim at a people's good, but they don't know what God designs 'em for. They don't know whether they are sent with Isaiah's message. God bid Ezekiel to speak His Word whether they would hear or whether they would forbear.

USE OF AWAKENING. This use is for ungodly men to seriously consider these things:

By so opposing God, you won 't hinder Him. You do but fight against your own souls. God will be no loser by it; how great a loser will you be!

God's Word you have, and it shall obtain its end. You may depend upon it that one sermon that you hear, however regardless you are of its message, will not be lost as to God, though it is lost as to you.

If the Word of God isn't as the dew and rain to you, it will at last be as fire to burn up your roots.

Consider the many sermons you have neglected and lost. They are all remembered. God will see that they aren't lost as to His ends proposed in them.

USE OF EXHORTATION. Let the doctrine exhort you to hear the Word of God delivered by His messengers. Fix that as your aim in hearing, that you may be profited for your spiritual good. Attend to and weigh it. Remember and apply it to yourself.

Let it be your constant endeavor to obey. Obey the commands of God; hearken to His counsels; accept His calls; strive diligently with your own heart. Mix earnest and constant prayer with it.

Consider that if you hear, God will attain His end in you, obtaining your own happiness. And then consider to how much greater advantage you may regard the Word of God now than afterwards. You will regard it first or last.

13

Those Only Who Are Holy Are on the Way to Heaven

"And an highway shall be there and a way; and it shall be called the way of holiness; the unclean shall not pass over it." Isaiah 35:8

The book of Isaiah speaks so much of Christ, and gives forth a particular accent at the birth, life, miracles, and position, and of the gospel state, that it has been called a fifth gospel. In this chapter is contained a glorious prophecy of the evangelical state.

We have a description of the flourishing state of Christ's kingdom in the two first verses in the conversion and enlightening of the heathen, here compared to a wilderness state, a desert, solitary place. "The wilderness and the solitary place shall be glad for them, and the desert shall rejoice and blossom as the rose. It shall blossom abundantly and rejoice even with joy and singing. The glory of Lebanon shall be given unto it, the excellency of Carmel and Sharon. They shall see the glory of the Lord and the excellency of our God."

The great privileges and precious advantages of the gospel are seen in the five following verses wherein the

205

strength, the courage, the reward, the salvation, the sighs
and understanding, comforts and joys that are conferred
thereby are very aptly described and set forth: "Strengthen
ye the weak hands and confirm the feeble knees. Say to
them that are of a fearful heart, 'Be strong, fear not. Behold, your God will come with vengeance, even God with a
recompense; He will come and save you.' Then the eyes of
the blind shall be opened, and the ears of the deaf shall be
unstopped. Then shall the lame man leap as an hart, and
the tongue of the dumb sing; for in the wilderness shall
waters break out, and streams in the desert. And the
parched ground shall become a pool, and the thirsty land
springs of water, in the habitation of dragons where each
lay shall be grass with reeds and rushes."

And the nature of the gospel and way of salvation
therein are brought to light. The holy nature of it is seen
in verses 8–9: "And an highway shall be there, and it shall
be called the way of holiness. The unclean shall not pass
over it, but it shall be for those the wayfaring men, though
fools, shall not err therein. No lion shall be there, nor any
ravenous beast shall go up thereon. It shall not be found
there, but the redeemed shall walk thereon."

The joyful nature of it is seen in verse 10: "And the ransomed of the Lord shall return and come to Zion with
songs and everlasting joy upon their heads; they shall obtain joy and gladness, and sorrow and sighing shall flee
away."

Observe in our text, first, the subject spoken, that is,
the way to salvation: "An highway shall be there, and a
way." This highway is the common and only way to heaven;
for the way to heaven is but one. None ever get to heaven

except they walk in this way. Some men don't get to heaven one way and others another. It is one highway that is always traveled by these that obtain heaven.

It is the same narrow way that Christ tells us of. Some don't go to heaven in a broad way and others in a narrow, some in an easy and other in a difficult way, some in a way of self-denial and mortification and others in a way of enjoyment of their lusts and sinful pleasures, some up a hill and others down. But the way to heaven is the same; it is the highway here spoken of. There is only one highway or road and no bypaths that some few go to heaven in as exceptions from the rest.

If we seek never so diligently, we shall never find an easier way to heaven than that which Christ has revealed to us. We cannot find a broader way, but if we go to heaven, the way is so narrow that we must rub hard to get along and march forward. The kingdom of heaven must suffer violence; it must be taken by force or else it never will be taken at all. If we don't go by the footstep of the flock, we shall never find the place where Christ feeds and where He makes His flock to rest at noon.

It appears that the way here spoken of is the way of salvation by the last verse of the chapter. When speaking of this way, it is said, "The ransomed of the Lord shall return and come to Zion and God." Zion is the common appellation by which in the Old Testament the church, both militant and triumphant, is signified.

Second, in the words observe the holy nature of this way described, first, by the name by which it is called: "the way of holiness." "And it shall be called the way of holiness." Second, by the holiness of those who travel in it, and its purity from those who are unclean or unholy: "the unclean shall not pass over it." No wicked person shall ever travel in this way of holiness. To the same purpose is the next verse: "no lion shall be there, nor any ravenous beast shall go up therein; it shall not be found there." That is, none of the wicked men of this world, who are like lions or ravenous beasts more than like men in their eager raging and lustful appetites and evil affections, or by their insatiable covetousness are like hungry wolves, are violently set upon the world and will have it whether by right or by wrong; or who make themselves like ravenous beasts by their proud, invidious, malicious dispositions, which are directly contrary to a Christian spirit and temper. They are more like wild beasts than Christians; they are wrongful and injurious, are all for themselves and for satisfying their own appetites and care nothing for the wishes of others. Their fellow men, who are of the same blood, make a God of their bellies and therein resemble tigers and wolves.

Now, says the prophet, "None such shall go upon this highway to Zion. Such unclean and ravenous beasts shall not be found there; no, but the redeemed shall walk there and the redeemed of the Lord shall return and come to Zion." This way is the way of holiness and is not to be defiled by wicked persons. Revelation 21:27 will serve well for an explication of these words: "And there shall in no wise enter into it anything that defileth, neither that whatsoever worketh abomination as maketh a lie, but they which are written in the Lamb's book of life."

DOCTRINE: Those only who are holy are on the way to heaven.

Many are not sensible enough of the necessity of holiness in order to salvation. Everyone hopes for heaven, but if everyone who hoped for heaven ever got there, heaven by this time would have been full of murderers, adulterers, common swearers, drunkards, thieves, robbers, and licentious debauchers. It would have been full of all manner of wickedness, and wicked men, such as the earth abounds with at this day. There would have been those who are no better than wild beasts, howling wolves, and poisonous serpents, yea, devils incarnate, as Judas was.

What a wicked place would the highest heaven have been, that pure, undefiled light and glorious place. The heavenly temple would be as the temple of Jerusalem was in Christ's time, a den of thieves. And the royal palace of the Most High, the holy metropolis of the creation, would be turned into a mere hell. There would be no happiness there for those who are holy. What a horrible, dreadful confusion there would be if the glorious presence of God the Father, the glorified Lamb of God, and the heavenly Dove, the Spirit of all grace and origin of all holiness, the spotless, glorified saints, the holy angels and wicked men, beasts and devils were all mixed up together.

Therefore it behooves us all to be sensible of the necessity of holiness in order to salvation, of the necessity of real, hearty, and sincere inward and spiritual holiness, such as will stand by us forever and will not leave us at death so that sinners may not be so foolish as to entertain hopes of heaven except they intend forthwith so far above repentance and reformation of heart and life. Wherefore this is what we are now upon, to show the necessity of holiness; and this we shall do in these three things: (1) show what holiness is; (2) that these who do not have it are not on the way to heaven; and (3) the reasons why it must be so.

QUESTION 1. What is holiness?

ANSWER. I shall answer this question in three things that fully comprehend no nature of holiness, that are not in themselves distinct or parts of holiness, but the same thing in a different light to give us the fuller understanding of it. First, holiness is a conformity of the heart and the life unto God. Whatever outward appearance men may make by their external actions, as if they were holy, yet if it does not proceed from a most inward, hearty, and sincere holiness within, it is nothing. Amaziah did that which was right in the sight of the Lord, but not with a perfect heart. All that he did was not acceptable to God who searches the hearts and tries the reins of the children of men, and must be worshipped in Spirit and in truth.

And whatever holiness they may pretend to have in their hearts, whatever hypocritical pangs of affection they may have had, it is all to no purpose except it manifests itself in the holiness of their lives and conversation. James 1:26–27: "If any man among you seem to be religious and bridleth not his tongue, but deceiveth his own heart, this man's religion is vain. Pure religion and undefiled before God and the Father is this, to visit the fatherless in their affliction, and to keep himself unspotted from the world." And in 2:18: "Yea, a man may say, 'Thou hast faith and I have works.' Show me thy faith without thy works and I will show thee my faith by my works." And in verses 19–20: "Thou believest that there is one God. Thou dost well; the devils also believe and tremble. But will thou know, O vain man, that faith without works is dead." So that there must be a conformity of both heart and life to God in order to true holiness.

Holiness is the image of God, His likeness in him who is holy. By being conformed unto God is not meant a conformity to Him in His eternity, infinity, or infinite power—these are Gods inimitable and incommunicable attributes—but a conformity to His will whereby he wills things that are just, right, and truly excellent and lovely, whereby he wills real perfection and goodness, and properly abhors everything that is really evil, unjust, and unreasonable.

And it is not only a willing as God wills, but also doing as He does, in acting holily, justly, wisely, and mercifully like Him. It must become natural thus to be and thus to act; it must be the constant inclination and new nature of the soul. It is a conformity to Jesus Christ. Christ Jesus is perfectly conformed unto God, for He is God. He is His express image. Now Christ is nearer to us in some respects than to God the Father for He is our Mediator and is more conversant with us. John 1:18: "No man hath seen God at any time; the only begotten Son who is in the bosom of the Father, He hath declared Him." Jesus Christ has been with us in the flesh, and as one of us He appeared in the form of a servant. And we have seen His holiness highly shining forth in all His actions. We have seen His holy life; we have a copy drawn and an example set for us.

Now holiness is a conformity unto this copy. He who copies Jesus Christ after that copy that He has set for us and that is delivered to us by the evangelists is holy; he who diligently observes the life of Christ in the new instance

need not be at a loss to know what holiness is. Christ
commands us to follow His example. Matthew 11:29:
"Take My yoke upon you and learn of Me, for I am meek
and lowly in heart and ye shall find rest unto your souls."

Have you ever read the four gospels, and did you not
observe in the life of Christ wonderful instances of humility, love for God, love for religion, wonderful instances of
zeal for God's glory, steadfastness in resisting temptations,
entire trust and reliance on God, strict observance to all
His commands, amazing instances of condescension, humility, meekness, lowliness, love for men, love for His enemies, charity, and patience? Why, this is holiness when we
imitate Christ in these things.

Holiness is a conformity to God's laws and commands.
When all God's laws without exception are written in our
hearts, then are we holy. If you can go along with David in
Psalm 119, when he speaks of his love and delight for
God's law in your own experience; when a man feels in
some good measure what David declares concerning himself towards the law of God, then may God's law be said to
be written in his heart. By God's law I mean all His precepts and commands, especially as they are delivered to us
in the gospel, which is the fulfillment of the law of God. If
you feel Christ's sermon upon the mount engraven on the
fleshly tables of your hearts, you are truly sanctified. Of
those that are sanctified, the new covenant is written in
their hearts, of which the Prophet Jeremiah speaks in
Jeremiah 31:31 and 33: "Behold, the days come, saith the
Lord, that I will make a new covenant with the house of
Israel and with the house of Judah. This shall be My covenant that I will make with the house of Israel after these

days, saith the Lord. I will put My laws in their inward parts and write it in their hearts. And I will be their God, and they shall be My people."

The commands and precepts that God has given us are all pure, perfect, and holy. They are the holiness of God in writing. And when the soul is conformed to them, they have holiness of God upon their hearts. 2 Corinthians 3:3: "For as much as ye are manifestly declared to be the epistle of Christ manifested by us, written not with ink, but with the Spirit of the living God; not in tables of stone, but in the fleshly tables of the heart." When the soul is molded and sanctified according to the image of God, the example of Christ, and the rule of the gospel, then it is holy and not else.

Those who do not have this holiness are not in the way to heaven. Those who are not thus conformed to God, to Christ, and God's commands are not in the way to heaven and happiness; they are not traveling that road. The road they are in will never bring them there. Whatever hopes and expectations they may have, they will never reach heaven to eternity except they alter their course, turn about and steer another course. Christ said that it was easier for a camel to go through the eye of a needle than for a rich man to enter into heaven, but yet He left it absolutely possible with God that it might be. But He said positively and without exception that unless a man is born again he cannot see the kingdom of God. None but those who are holy are in the way to heaven, whatever profession they may make, whatever church they may be in. For "in Christ Jesus neither circumcision availeth anything nor uncircumcised, but a new creature." Whatever externals of religion they may perform, however constant they may be in attending on public and family worship, and live outwardly moral lives; yea, what is more, if they preach with the tongues of men and angels, though they could prophesy and understand all mysteries and all knowledge, and though they have faith that they can remove mountains, though they bestow all and though they give their goods to feed the poor, give their bodies to be burned, yet if they have not charity or holiness (which is the same thing, for by "charity" is intended love to God as well as men), though they have and do all these things yet they are nothing. They are as a sounding brass or tinkling cymbal (see 1 Corinthians 13).

It is good that we should be thoroughly convinced of the most absolute and indispensable necessity of a real, spiritual, active, virtual, yea immortal holiness. So we shall now give the reasons why none who are not holy can be in the way to heaven, and why those who never are so can never obtain the happiness thereof:

REASON 1. 'Tis contrary to God's justice to make a wicked man eternally happy. God is a God of infinite justice, and His justice, to speak after the manner of men, obliges Him to punish sin eternally. Sin must be punished; the sins of all men must be punished; if the sinner retains his sin and it is not washed of by the blood of Christ, and he is not purified and sanctified and made holy, it must be purified upon him. If he is sanctified, his sin has been already punished in the passion of Christ; but if not it will remain to be punished in his eternal pain and misery. For God has said that He is a holy and jealous God and is by no means willing to clear the guilty. It is reckoned amongst the rest of God's attributes that He proclaims in Exodus 34:7 and Numbers 14:18.

REASON 2. 'Tis impossible by reason of God's holiness that anything should be united to God and brought to the enjoyment of Him that is not holy. How it is possible that a God of infinite holiness, who is perfect and hates sin with perfect hatred, who is infinitely lovely and excellent, could embrace in His arms a filthy, abominable creature, a hideous, detestable monster, more hateful than a toad and more poisonous than a viper? But so hateful, bad, and abominable is every unsanctified man, even the best hypocrite and most painted sepulchers of them all.

How impossible it is that this should be, that such loathsome beings, the picture of the devil, should be united to God, should be a member of Christ, a child of God's, made happy in the enjoyment of His love and the smiles of His benevolence, should be in God and God in them? For it is as impossible that God should love sin as it is for Him to cease to be; and it is as impossible for Him to love a wicked man who does not have his sin purified, and it is as impossible for that wicked man to enjoy the happiness of heaven except God loves him—for the happiness of heaven consists in the enjoyment of God's love.

REASON 3. It would defile heaven and interrupt the happiness of the saints and angels; it would defile that holy place, the Holy of Holies, and would frighten the sanctified spirits, and obstruct them in their delightful ecstasies of devotion and praise; it would quite confound the heavenly society. How would one unsanctified person interrupt their happiness and fill those regions all over with the loathsome stench of sin and filthiness.

REASON 4. The nature of sin necessarily infers misery. The soul that remains sinful must of necessity remain miserable; for it is impossible there should be any happiness where such a hateful thing as sin reigns and bears rule. Sin is the most cruel tyrant that ever ruled; it seeks nothing but the misery of its subjects. As in the very keeping of God's commands there is great reward, so in the very breaking of them there is great punishment.

Sin is a woeful confusion and dreadful disorder within the soul whereby everything is put out of place. Reason is trampled under foot and passion advanced in its place; conscience is dethroned and abominable cults reign. As long as it is so, there will unavoidably be a dreadful confusion and perturbation in the mind; the soul will be full of wars, perplexities, uneasiness, storms, and frights. And thus it must necessarily be to all eternity except the Spirit of God puts all right. So that if it were possible that God should desire to make a wicked man happy while he is wicked, the nature of the thing would not allow of it, but it would be simply and absolutely impossible.

Thus I have given some reasons of the doctrine why it must be that those who are not holy cannot be in the way to heaven. Many more reasons might be offered which the time will not allow to take notice of at this time; but these alone would have been enough to show us that none but those who are holy ever obtain a crown of glory even if God had not expressly said that without holiness no man should see the Lord.

Application

USE OF INFERENCE. If it is so that none but those who are holy are in the way to heaven, how many poor creatures are there who think they are in the way to heaven who are not? There are many who think that they are undoubtedly in the way to heaven and without question shall enter there at last who do not have the least grain of true holiness, who manifest none in their lives and conversations, of whom we may be certain that either they have no holiness at all or that which they have is a dormant, inactive sort, which is in effect to be certain that there is none. There are a great many others who are not so definitively and plainly perceived, who have nothing but what is external, the shell without the kernel. Great multitudes are of these two kinds.

What a pitiable, miserable condition are they in, to step out of this world into an uncertain eternity with an expectation of finding themselves exceedingly happy and blessed in the highest heavens, and all at once find themselves deadened and deceived, finding themselves in the bottomless pit.

USE OF TRIAL. If none are in the way to heaven but those who are holy, let us try and examine ourselves by this doctrine to see where we are and whether or not we are in the way to heaven, to know which way we are going, whether towards Canaan or Egypt, whether towards heaven or hell; for if we think ourselves in the road to heaven and are going to the place of torment all the while, and continue deceived, without doubt we shall perish and fire and brimstone will undeceive us. If we find ourselves in the broad way to destruction, how dare we take a step further.

If we would know whether we are holy as not, let us try ourselves by these following things:

1. Meditate on the holiness of God and see if you cannot see a conformity, a likeness in your mind. There is no likeness or comparison in degree; but yet we do not speak of this. There is a likeness in nature between God and the soul of the believer. The holy soul, when it thinks and meditates upon God's nature, finds a pleasure and delights because there is agreeableness in his new nature to the divine perfections. If those who think themselves in the way to heaven who are unholy in the meantime in their hearts, if such would compare themselves and their nature to the holy nature of God, such a glorious light as the holiness of God would quickly discover their unsoundness.

2. See if you can see any resemblance in your life to the life of Christ. It is not supposed that ever any copy came near to this original, nor ever will, but yet they may perceive whether the same spirit, the same temper and disposition in a lesser degree is in them that was manifested by the life and conversation of Jesus Christ.

3. Is there an agreeableness between your souls and the Word of God? The Bible is the epistle of Christ that He has written to us. Now, if the same epistle is also written in our hearts that is written in the Scripture, it may be found out by comparing. Do you have love for all God's commands and a respect for them in your actions? Is it your delight to obey and hearken to the will of God? Do you obey them of choice? Is it what you would choose to do if God had not threatened to punish the breach of them?

4. Do you find by a comparison a likeness and agreeableness between your hearts and lives and the hearts and lives of these holy men that we afford were such by the Word of God? Do you walk with God as Enoch did? Do you distinguish yourselves by your piety in the midst of wicked examples, as Noah did? And when you read the lives of Abraham, Isaac, Jacob, Moses, and the prophets, wherein holiness is drawn to the life, you may, viewing so exact a picture, discover whether you have the root of the matter in you, though it is more obscured in you than in them. When we read the Psalms of David we may clearly see what his belief was by that spirit that is breathed there; when we read the epistles of the apostles we may know what is a truly evangelical spirit, and whether such a spirit reigns in our souls.

5. Do you in a measure imitate the saints and angels in heaven? They sound their praises to the glory of God; they love Him above all things, are daily enamored with the beauties of Jesus Christ, entirely love one another, and hate sin; and those who are holy on earth have also a resemblance and are imitators of them. They are of a heavenly temper, are of heavenly lives.

USE OF EXHORTATION. Let the doctrine exhort all to holiness. You have heard what holiness is, and of the necessity of it, the absolute necessity in order to escaping hell, what we must have or die forever. Sin must be forsaken forever. Now nothing is so necessary to us as holiness; other things may be necessary, and things that are necessary men will strive for with all their might if there is a probability of obtaining them. How much more is that to be sought after without which we shall fare infinitely worse than die ten thousand deaths?

This is motive enough without any other, for what can be a greater motive than necessity? But consider that if it were not necessary, the amiable and excellent nature of it is enough to make it worth the most earnest seeking after.

Holiness is a most beautiful, lovely thing. Men are apt to drink in strange notions of holiness from their childhood, as if it were a melancholy, morose, sour, and unpleasant thing; but there is nothing in it but what is sweet and ravishingly lovely. 'Tis the brighter beauty and amiableness, vastly above all other beauties; 'tis a divine beauty, makes the soul heavenly, and far purer than anything here on earth. This world is like mire and filth and defilement to the soul that is sanctified. 'Tis of a sweet, lovely, delightful, serene, calm, and still nature.

Christian holiness is above all the heathen virtue of a mere bright and pure nature; it is more serene, calm, peaceful, and delightful. What a sweet calmness, what a calm ecstasy it brings to the soul. Of what a meek and humble nature is true holiness, how peaceful and quiet. How it changes the soul and makes it more pure, more bright, and more excellent than other beings.

14

Christ Is a Person of Transcendent Worthiness in the Sight of God

" For unto which of the angels said He at any time, 'Thou art My Son; this day have I begotten thee?' " Hebrews 1:5

(Preached in March 1736)

A principle design of the apostle in this epistle is to show the excellency of the gospel, or of the new dispensation inspired by Christ, over the law of the old legal dispensation by Moses. And the argument that he begins with is the superior excellency and glory of Christ, the Person through whose bonds alone it was delivered, and particularly His being more excellent than the prophets, those by whom He spoke under the Old Testament, and more excellent than the angels. It was chiefly by the ministration of prophets and angels that God gave revelations under the Old Testament.

In the first place he mentions the prophets and compares Christ with them. In the first two verses of the epistle we read: "God, who at sundry times and in divers manners spake in time past unto the fathers by the prophets, hath in these last days spoken unto us by his Son."

221

And next he proceeds to compare Christ with the angels, because of old God revealed His mind by their ministration, as in the second verse of the next chapter: "For if the word spoken by angels was steadfast, and every transgression and disobedience received a just recompense of reward. . . ." This was to show the excellency of the old dispensation, introduced by Christ, to the Old Testament, which was by the ministration of angels. In the seventh verse he mentions His excellency in His works, and the honor that God had put upon Him. He mentions His Excellency in Himself in that He upholds all things, and that He tasted death for our sins. This shows the favor that God had put upon Him in His exaltation, in His being set down at the right hand of the Majesty on High (8:2). In His exaltation God had put greater favor upon Him than even He did upon the angels; therefore it follows in verse 4: "Being made so much better than the angels as He hath by intent." God, thus putting greater honor upon Him than He ever did upon the angels, gave Him no more than this honor of being set above the angels than what was defined, and was no more than to the superior excellence of the name that properly belonged to Him by inheritance. And there in verse 5 of our text the apostle shows how Christ had by inheritance obtained a more excellent name than the angels. Therefore in the text observe true unity:

1. What that name is that Christ has by inheritance, that of the Son of God. God said unto Him, "Thou art My Son." God looked upon Him as worthy that He should thus accept Him and said, "Give Him this name."

2. How He obtained this name by inheritance, in that God had begotten Him. This name He did not have by

grace; it was not by a free adoption. This day had God begotten Him by eternal generation. It was what He was heir
of, to be called God's Son. The place here referred to by
the apostle, God had said this to Christ in Psalm 2, in the
beginning of which psalm is set forth how that man shall
set Christ as naught, how the heathen and the people
imagine a vain thing, how the kings of the earth set themselves against God, and how the rich take counsel together
against the Lord and against Christ. In verse 7 what honor
God puts upon Christ: "I will declare the decree: 'The
Lord hath said unto Me, "Thou art My Son; this day have I
begotten Thee." ' "

3. We may observe in the text how Christ herein was
distinguished from the angels: "For unto which of the
people said He in like manner. . . ." The angels are beings
of great excellency and dignity; they are represented in
Scripture in excellence, in strength and wisdom. They are
as a tribune of fire and are called by Him honorable titles
in dominion, principalities, and powers. But these were
not thought worthy in the sight of God of such an honorable name as Jesus Christ was. He at no time accepted
them as He did Him. Indeed, the angels are called the sons
of God in Job 38:7, and so are the saints, but not in like
manner. God at no time says to them after such a manner,
"Thou art My Son." This shows plainly that Christ is God's
Son in a familiar and transcendent manner in that He is a
natural Son and heir. He is His Son in a way by Himself
alone and insomuch that My Creator is a Son of God.

**DOCTRINE: Christ is a person of transcen-
dent worthiness in the sight of God.**

God looks upon Him as a Person of exceeding dignity, enough so that of all the creatures in heaven and earth there are none found so worthy in God's sight as Jesus Christ. He is the firstborn of God, and has the preeminence above all, as in Colossians 1:15–18. This was remarkably testified in the vision that John had of the book sealed with seven seals that represents the book of God's decrees. John tells us in Revelation 5:2–3 that he saw a strange angel proclaiming with a loud voice, "Who is worthy to open the book and to loose the seals thereof? And no man in heaven nor on earth, neither under the earth, was able to open the book, neither to look thereon." No one else was found worthy; the Lord, the Lion of the tribe of Judea and the tribe of David was found worthy to do it. And see how on that occasion the hosts of heaven fall down before Him and sing a new song, saying, "Thou art worthy to take the book and to open the seals thereof."

In handling this doctrine I would do two things: First, I would show on what account Christ is a Person of such worthiness in the sight of God, and, second, show what it is that God accounts Him worthy of.

I would show that Christ is, in God's sight a Person of exceeding worthiness, first, on the account of what He is, and, second, on the account of what He has done.

First, I would show what His worthiness is in these respects, and, second, what God looked upon Him as being worthy of. And I would do this in the following method:

I would show how that Christ is a person of exceeding worthiness in the sight of God on the account of what He is, and on the account of what He has done.

Therefore Christ is in the sight of God a Person of transcendent worthiness on the account of what He is.

Christ is a Person of transcendent worthiness in the sight of God on the account of His excellence. The excellence and glory of Christ, however light it is made of by some of the children of men, yet is in the sight of God intimately great and a Person of infinite worthiness in His esteem on that account. Christ is possessed of all the excellence and glory of God. The Father Himself has every divine perfection; and therefore He is said to be the express or perfect image of the Father.

God the Father, in beholding the Son, beholds all His own glory; and therefore, as God has an infinite value for His own glory and beauty, so He has an infinite value for His Son, for He sees it all in Him, for He is the brightness of His glory as 'tis said in verse 3 of our text. Christ is of an infinitely glorious and excellent nature because He has the divine nature and essence. God greatly values His own image of His own holiness in the angels; and not only so, but when it is imperfect, as it is in the saints. But if God so values a little, dim reflection, and a faint shadow of His own beauty, how may we conclude that He values that image that contains His very essence? If He so values a faintly reflected ray, how may we conclude He sits by the infinite Fountain of Light Himself? The saints on earth have but little of the excellence of Christ; yea, the saints and angels in heaven can comprehend but little. But God has it all, and that perfectly, perpetually, and eternally.

Christ is a Person of transcendent worthiness in the sight of God because He is His Son, because of His relation to Him. God has an infinite value for His Son as He is in an infinitely honorable relationship to Him.

The angels and saints stand in a near and honorable relation to God, but the relation of Christ to Him is infinitely above theirs, or that of any creature. Children are dear to their parents, and Christ is dear and honorable in the sight of God because He is His Son. And therefore in Scripture Christ's being His Son and being beloved are so often joined together. He is called God's beloved Son.

This ground of God's great esteem of His Son is intimated in the text: "Thou art My Son; this day have I begotten Thee." That is monitored as the ground of God's valuing and honoring Christ, and so much more than the angels; hereby Christ is an heir of the esteem of the Father because He has begotten Him. He may challenge the Father's infinite esteem and to be looked upon as infinitely worthy in His sight by His due inheritance. Thus Christ is a Person of transcendent worthiness in the sight of God on the account of what He is.

I proceed now to show that Christ is worthy in the sight of God on the account of this worthiness, and would mention at this time but four things:

1. God accounts Him worthy to be infinitely loved and delighted by Him. Christ is the object of the love of God as no created being is. The streams of divine love may flow out towards other objects, but God pours forth the infinite fountain wholly upon Jesus Christ. God's infinite love is in many respects towards the creature; but the infinite love of God is exceedingly towards Christ infinitely. God's whole essence is love, and it does, as it were, go wholly towards Jesus Christ.

Hence Christ is called "the Beloved" in Ephesians 1:6: "To the praise and glory of His grace, wherein He hath made us accepted in the Beloved." Hence God the Father proclaimed with an incredible voice from heaven at Christ's baptism in Matthew 3:17: "This is My beloved Son, in whom I am well pleased." And there is the same voice again at His transfiguration in chapter 17:5. Hence Christ says in John 3:35, "The Father loveth the Son." And God, in Isaiah 42:1 calls Christ "Mine elect in whom My soul delighteth." It was probably chiefly for this reason that it was so ordered in Providence that David, the principal type of Christ, was called by that name that signified "beloved."

The infinite happiness of God seems to consist in the delight He has in His Son Jesus Christ. God's happiness consists in beholding His own beauty and loving Him so; but He beholds Himself and His own beauty in His express image and the brightness of His glory. Hence this is the account He gives of Himself, what He was before the world was created, and even from eternity. Proverbs 8:30: "Then was I by Him, as one brought up with Him; and I was daily His delight, rejoicing always before Him."

2. Christ is in the sight of God worthy to be the Heir of all things. As He is the Son of God, so He is God's heir. And as He is the only begotten Son, He is the Heir of all that God possesses, as Abraham gave Isaac all that he had, who is called Abraham's only son. In the second verse of our context, "He hath in these last days spoken to us by His Son, whom He hath appointed Heir of all things." As Christ has built all things, so the house is His (Hebrews 3:3–4).

Christ is looked upon by God as worthy to inherit the kingdom and government of the world, to be appointed as mighty and absolute Lord of heaven, as the owner of all. And therefore He has given all things to Him, as Christ says in John 3:35, "The Father loveth the Son and hath given all things into His hands."

3. God accounts Him worthy of the same honor with Himself. This is the declared word of God, that all should honor Christ as they honor Him. So John 5:23: "That all men should honor the Son even as they honor the Father." God has declared to all men His will, that Christ should be the object of divine worship as He Himself and that even from the highest and most excellent of creations. Or, in the next verse to the text, "And again, when He bringeth the first begotten into the world, He saith, 'And let all the angels of God worship Him.' "

4. He was thought worthy to be appointed to the great office of a Mediator between God and sinful men. The office was that which no creature was found equal to. No mere creature in heaven or on earth was found worthy to undertake the work of the redemption of sinners. It was too great a work for any of them; none but Christ was found of sufficient worthiness to stand between God and sinners. So then God might, on His account and for His sake, be at peace with them who had offended the divine majesty and done that which was infinitely contrary to God's holiness.

But the only begotten Son of God who was in the bosom of the Father, He was thought worthy and in all respects sufficient for the undertaking, and therefore was appointed thereto. He was chosen when all others were rejected. He was anointed and sent into the world to do this work.

But I proceed now in the second place to show that Christ is a Person of transcendent worthiness in the sight of God on the account of what He has done, and particularly what He has done in the work of redemption. This was the great work to which He was set apart and anointed, whence He is called the Messiah or Christ, which words, the one in Hebrew and the other in the Greek, signify "the anointed." And this work Christ has undertaken and performed to the acceptance of the Father. And God looks on what He has done in this work as being of infinite dignity and value, and that in the following accounts:

1. What He has done He did through so great humiliation and suffering. It was a great thing because it was so glorious a Person who did it. We have already considered the worthiness of Christ in Himself; and the worthiness of the Person puts an infinite value upon what He did in God's account.

Deeds of love and respect towards us are of greater value in our account from a person of greater dignity and excellence. So are deeds of love and respect towards God of greater value from those who are of great value and excellence in His eyes. The love of one who is excellent and honorable in God's eyes is proportionately of greater value to God than one who is less worthy because he who is of great dignity in his love gives God more. So far as he loves, so far he devotes himself; he is loving and gives his heart. But the heart of one who is of greater dignity is worth more than one who is of lesser dignity. Hence what

Christ did in what He offered to God is justly of greater
worth in God's eyes in proportion to the dignity of His
Person.

2. Jesus Christ is of infinite dignity and value on account of the great humiliation and suffering through
which it was done. Christ exceedingly humbled and abased
Himself in doing what He did for our redemption. It was a
great thing in God's eyes for a person of great glory so to
abase Himself. It was a great thing in God's sight for Him
who was so high in Himself to take our nature upon Him
in such mean and low circumstances. It was yet a far
greater thing for Him to subject Himself to such an ignominious, painful, and accursed death, to make His soul an
offering for sin and to become a victim to wrath.

It was a great thing for Him to wade along through
such a train of difficulties, reproach, and suffering for so
many years together on this earth. No creature, in anything that ever they have done in all their good deeds, ever
performed anything through so much difficulty and suffering as Christ has done; and if they had gone through as
much suffering as He, it would not have been a matter of
such consideration. It would have been an infinitely less
thing; there would have been infinitely less humiliation in
it than there was in Christ for the degree of humiliation is
to be measured from the height of dignity and glory that
He originally possessed. But this height was infinite, and
therefore His humiliation was infinitely greater than of any
creature if they had suffered as much, yea, if they had suffered a thousand times as much.

But Christ was not only infinitely greater and higher in
Himself, but suffered immensely more than ever any went

through in any good deed; and therefore what He did was proportionately greater, and of greater account in the sight of God. This is what the heavenly hosts insist upon as what renders Christ worthy. Revelation 5:12: "Worthy is the Lamb that was slain."

3. What Christ did through so much humiliation was out of respect for God. Christ therein testified infinite regard for the honor of God's majesty, and that in two ways: First, as it was done to render the sinner's escape consistent with the honor of His majesty, that when He loved sinful men and desired that they might escape, He would rather infinitely humble Himself than that the escape of the sinner should be injurious to the honor of His majesty. Second, as it was done out of obedience to God's commands; for all that He did and all that He went through in His state of humiliation was out of obedience to God. His laying down His life was in obedience to Him. John 10:17–18: "Therefore doth My Father love Me, because I lay down My life. . . . This commandment have I received of My Father." Philippians 2:6–8: "Who, being in the form of God, thought it not robbery to be equal with God, but made himself of no reputation, and took upon him the form of a servant, and was made in the likeness of men. And being found in fashion as a man, he humbled himself, and became obedient unto death, even the death of the cross."

Here He testified an infinite love for God, and respect for His authority, that so great a Person would be obedient to God's commands, though it cost Him so much, He would obey; and He infinitely humbled Himself so to do. And what makes His great respect for God's authority the

more evident is that He would thus obey though He was
originally under no obligation to obedience. He was in nature equal with God and not subject to Him any otherwise
than He voluntarily put Himself in a state of subjection.

4. What Christ did in the work of redemption has a
transcendent excellence in it, as He therefore exercised
and manifested infinite love and mercy to fallen man.
What Christ did was exceedingly excellent on this account;
for as God is a God of infinite grace and has infinite delight in His own attributes, so He has infinite delight in His
grace. Therefore He greatly delighted in what Christ did,
as He therein exercised infinite grace in so transcendent a
manner.

5. What Christ did is most worthy in the sight of God
on the account of the infinite good that is the fruit of it.
Exceeding glory to the name of God is the fruit of this.
Christ came into the world for this, to glorify the Father;
and therefore that was the request that Christ made when
He was going to Jerusalem to be crucified. John 12:28: "Father, glorify Thy name." He suffered and was made a sacrifice for sin for the glory of God's vindictive justice; and He
obeyed for the honor of God's law. He glorified all God's
attributes. By what He did in the work of our redemption,
He has brought more glory to the name of God than all
the saints and angels in heaven and on earth put together.
And besides that is infinite good to the creature; that is the
fruit of what He has done. On this account God delights
in what He has done; and therefore the saints in heaven
exalt Him as worthy on the account of the great good that
they have received. Revelation 5:9: "Thou art worthy to

take the book and to open the seal, for Thou wast slain and hast redeemed us."

I proceed now to show what God has accounted Christ worthy of on account of what He has done, as under the former heading are fulfilled what God thought Him worthy of on account of what He is. There are two things especially that God has esteemed Christ worthy of on the account of what He did in the affair of redemption.

1. God, on the account of what He has done, has judged Christ worthy of His own exaltation, that exaltation and glory to what God the Father has advanced Christ as God-man since His death as a reward for what He did in the work of our redemption—the glory that was begun in His reformation and performed in His ascension and sitting at the right hand of God in heaven and continued in His reigning there over angels and men, heaven and earth as our Mediator, and that will receive its most illustrious manifestation in His judging the world at the last day. This is a reward that was promised Him in the eternal covenant of redemption for what He was to do and suffer in that world in the work of redemption. Philippians 2:8–11: "He humbled Himself and became obedient unto death, even the death on the cross. Wherefore God hath highly exalted and given Him a name which is above every name, of things in heaven and things on the earth, that at the name of Jesus every knee should bow and that every tongue should confess that Jesus Christ is Lord to the glory of God the Father."

Therefore the glory of Christ's exaltation is what the heavenly hosts ascribe to Him or what He is worthy of on the account of His sufferings. Revelation 5:12: "Worthy is the Lamb that was slain to receive power and riches and wisdom and strength and honor and glory and blessing." When Christ's exaltation was begun, then God put that honor upon Him.

In the text, His exaltation began with His resurrection, and then it was in a special manner that God said to Him, as in the text, "Thou art My Son; this day have I begotten Thee," as the words are applied. This same Apostle Paul, in Acts 13:33, wrote: "God hath fulfilled the same unto us, their children, in that He hath raised up Jesus again, as it is also written in the second Psalm, 'Thou art My Son; this day have I begotten Thee.' "

2. On the account of what Christ has done, God accounts Him worthy that all who are His should be called and accepted and glorified on His account. Such is the worthiness of what He has done that God doesn't only look upon Him as worthy on that account to exalt Him so, but also that all who are His should be delivered and made happy; for His sake to call and bring savingly home all who are written on His heart, and whom He has set His eternal love upon.

And this was part of what Christ had respect to in doing and suffering, in what He did, to accept all and justify them, however great their sin and unworthiness has been, let their guilt be never so great in God's sight, and to glorify those who are justified and have His righteousness, and to advance to eternal honor and blessedness. This was part of the joy that was set before Christ, that He had respect to in doing and suffering what He did.

This Christ's honor set open, and this was part of the reward that was promised to Him on the glorious account of redemption for His obedience and suffering in Isaiah 53:10: "When Thou shalt make His soul an offering for sin, He shall see His seed. He shall prolong His days, and the pleasure of the LORD shall prosper in His hand."

Christ, when He obeyed and died, did not obey and die as a private person, but as our representative. So when He was exalted, it was not as a private person, but as our Head. He took possession of glory in our name. He is risen and ascended as the first fruits. 1 Corinthians 15:23: "Christ the first fruits and afterwards they that are Christ's at His coming."

The whole reward that was promised for what Christ did and suffered may be summed up in this, the exaltation of Christ mystical, which includes both what is mentioned in this and foregoing particular. And exaltation includes the whole reward for what He did in His humiliation; but then it must be the whole Christ that is exalted, that is, both the Head and the members. When Christ mystical is thus wholly and completely glorified, then He will be in possession of the complete reward that God promised Him, and this whole reward God has thought Him worthy of and has promised Him, and will surely accomplish.

Inferences

1. Hence we may learn why God has spoken in His Word so much of His Son from the beginning of the world. God has surely insisted on His Word in all ages since man was upon the earth. He began to speak of Him adoringly. He had respect to Him in what was said to Noah. He spoke of Him again to Abraham, Isaac, and Jacob, again

to Moses. In all the law that was given by Moses respect was had to Christ. To typify Christ, all the furniture of the tabernacle and temple was to show Him. The histories that were written by holy men hold forth Christ to us. The persons and events that are the judges of their history evidently typify Christ and the things of Christ.

Christ is the main subject of the songs of inspired persons. The Book of Psalms that was penned by many persons in different ages is all of Christ. He is the great subject that the prophets wrote of; though they speak of other things, yet He is the main drift. Christ is the great subject of the glorious gospel, and those more clear revelations given in the New Testament dispensation.

Now our doctrine may lead us to one reason why God has spoken so much of Christ, and has so dwelt on this subject from age to age. It is because He is a Person of such transcendent worthiness in His eyes. He has esteemed Him worthy to be the first subject of His Word.

That which men set way highly by and set their hearts much upon, that are they ready to speak much of.

2. Hence we may learn the reason why God has so much contrived to glorify His own Son, Jesus Christ. God has exceedingly laid Himself out to bring honor and glory to His Son. This God aimed at in creating the world, to glorify His Son. Hence we read that all things were created for Christ. Colossians 1:16: "All things were created by Him and for Him."

Hence also God has ordered that all things might be gathered together and brought home to Him. Ephesians 1:10: "That in the dispensation of the fullness of time He might gather together in one all things in Christ, both which are in heaven and which are on earth, even in Him." And hence He has appointed Him to be the great medium of all good to man, and to be all in all so that all might be revealed by Him, the great Prophet and Light of the world, and all might be procured by Him, the Great High Priest, and He might be conferred by Him as the Great King. He has made Him not only the Redeemer of the world but the Judge of the world.

Hence God has out all things under Christ's feet and made Him to be Head over all things, so that nothing is accepted but what is subjected to Him by God Himself. Hebrews 2:7–8: "Thou crownedst Him with glory and honor and didst set Him over the works of Thine hands. Thou hast put all things in subjection under Him." He left nothing that is not put under Him. And so we are told in Ephesians 1:21 that God has set Him far above all principalities, powers, might, and dominion, and every name that is named not only in this world, but also in that which is to come. And He has ordered it so that Christ in all things should have the preeminence. Colossians 1:18: "And He is the head of the body, the church, who is the beginning, the First-born from the dead, that in all things He might have the preeminence."

And the reason of all this contriving and dispersing for the glory of Christ is that which was told in verse 12, that Christ is a Person of such transcendent worthiness in God's sight.

3. Hence we learn why it is so displeasing to God, and so fatal to the souls of men, when they ascribe that glory to themselves that belongs to Christ. God manifests it in His Word to be very displeasing and ravenous to man when

they ascribe the glory of Solomon to themselves or to any mere creature by trusting in them. Jeremiah 17:5: "Cursed be he that trusts in man and that maketh these his own." He has often taught the fatalness of men's trusting in their own strength and righteousness. And the reason for it is that this detracts from the glory that is done to His Son. Men assure themselves of that which is the prerogative of Jesus, which God will not endure since Christ is a Person of such exceeding worthiness in His sight.

And hence we may learn how admirable to God and fatal to man these doctrines are that set man up and ascribe much to man's power and ability, and to man's obedience. God will not endure such doctrines, or He won't suffer the glory due to His Son alone should be given to any other.

Let all therefore be hence warned to take heed of these things. See that you don't exalt yourself in your own righteousness and strength. God won't bear this. Be aware that you don't. God will be no other than a condemning fire if you do. Avoid and abominate more than a toad or viper those doctrines that set up man's strength and righteousness in the affair of salvation if you would not bring down the thunder of divine vengeance on your head.

4. Hence we may learn the safety of trusting in Jesus Christ for salvation. If He is a Person of such exceeding worthiness in God's sight, then doubtless it is a safe thing coming to God in His name. If we come in Christ and under His covenant, there is no danger of being rejected; for Christ is so worthy in God's eyes that He never will reject Him. It is impossible that He should. If we can have Him to be our Mediator, we shall have what is sufficient that will

certainly prevail. His worthiness is sufficient to make 'em very clean.

However unworthy we have been, Christ is so worthy in the sight of God. That is enough to make up for our unworthiness, let us be as unworthy as we will. His great worthiness in the sight of God makes His blood of infinite value, and of sufficient value without a doubt to atone for the sins of the worst of us all. We have heard of the worthiness of what Christ has done in God's sight, and what has been said is certain. All our unworthiness is great. If we come to Christ, we'll be smothered up in His worthiness as little meteors are smothered up in the abundant light of the body of the sun.

Christ calls and invites everyone to come to Him and faithfully promises that if we will come to Him, He will in no way cast us out. He will undertake for us, shed His blood for us; before God He will intercede for us, and His worthiness in the sight of God is such that there is no danger that Christ's intercession won't prevail, for God hears Him always (John 11:42). Let sinners who are concerned for their souls hence take heed to look to Christ, and come and cast themselves on Him.

5. Hence we may learn the reason why God so highly resents persons rejecting Christ and setting Him at naught. This teaches us the ground of the exceeding sin of unbelief, that sin that is spoken of in Scripture as the greatest of all sins. John 3:18–19: "he who believeth not is condemned already because he hath not believed." John 16:8–9: "And when He is come, He will reprove the world of sin, and of righteousness, and of judgment. Of sin, because they believe not in Me."

They who live under the gospel and yet continue in unbelief reject the glorious Son of God. He is a stone that is set at naught by them. Whatever pretences and shows of respect they make towards Christ outwardly, they have no respect in their hearts for Him; they give Christ no room in their hearts; they don't look upon Him as worthy, and they have no time, respect, or esteem for Him, no manner of love for Him.

How highly may we conclude that God resents this, when men will not trust a person of such great dignity in His eyes, that He can come into the world and shed His precious blood. He comes with the blood and stands at their door and knocks from day to day, offering Himself and His benefits to poor, perishing sinners; and they bolt the door against Him. Surely God will resent such treatment of such a Person. His wrath shall not slumber towards these who do. This sin, without a doubt, will make their case more dreadful another day than that of the sinners of Sodom and Gomorrah, if Jesus so resents it when any do evilly treat the saints.

Let such consider that though they set Christ at naught, yet He shall be the Head of the corner; though you endeavor to break Christ's bonds asunder and cast His cords from you and say, "We will not have this man to rule over us," yet He who sits in the heavens shall have you in derision. He will speak to you in His wrath and vex you in His anger. He has set His king in His holy hill of Zion and has said to Him, "Rule Thou in the midst of Thine enemies," and He shall break them with a rod of iron as the vessels of wrath.

6. We may hence infer how worthy and honorable be-

lievers are in God's sight who are members of Jesus Christ. Such are in a most near relation to Him; they are of flesh of His flesh and bones of His bones (Ephesians 5:30). Their souls are espoused and married to Christ. Seeing that Christ is a Person of such infinite worthiness, doubtless God will look on His spouse as such. Isaiah 43:4: "Since thou wast precious in My sight, thou hast been honorable, and I will love thee."

And hence it is that the saints do their grand works and come to be entitled to a reward. God looks on them as honorable, and persons of great dignity in Christ; and hereby a value is put on what they do so that, notwithstanding the exceeding imperfections and pollutions there are in themselves, yet they shall have an exceedingly great, glorious, and eternal reward.

7. Last, if it is so, then hence we may learn the exceeding happiness of those who can say concerning Christ, "He is mine." As honorable and glorious a Person as He is, yet He is the possession of believers; they can say of Him, "He is mine and I am His." Indeed, how happy are they who are united to Christ, who have such a Friend, such a Portion, who have one for the Husband of their souls as He whom God sets such a high value upon.

God knows how to value things. He knows the true worth of them. And when He looks at Christ as a Person of such exceeding worthiness, He looks on Him as He is. Hence they who have the possessions of Jesus are blessed; they are happy indeed. They have cause to rejoice and will rejoice with unspeakable joy.

15

God Is a Being Possessed of the Most Absolutely Perfect Happiness

"Which in His times He shall show who is the blessed
and only Potentate." 1 Timothy 6:15

(Preached November 23, 1738)

The apostle concludes this epistle to Timothy with a most solemn charge to him to be faithful in that great work to which he was called. Whatever trials and persecutions he might be called to go through for it seems then to have been a time of persecution in that part of the churches of Christ where Timothy was, which the apostle has respect to in verse 12: "Fight the good fight of faith."

And then, in the most solemn manner, he enforces this charge from several things he tells him. He gives him this charge in the light of God, who quickens all things; he mentions His quickening all things to encourage Timothy to fight the good fight of the faith and to continue faithful in his work, though he should expose himself to death by it. If he should die in the service of Christ, God, who quickens all things, would quicken and raise him again.

The apostle further tells Timothy that he gives him this

242

charge before Jesus Christ who, before Pontius Pilate, witnessed a good confession. He puts him in mind of Christ professing the truth before His persecutors to exhort him to be faithful under persecution.

The next thing the apostle puts him in mind of to ensure this charge is the second coming of Christ. Verse 14: "That thou keep this commandment without spot, unrebukeable, until the appearing of our Lord Jesus Christ." Then come the words of the text: "which in His time He shall show who is the blessed and only Potentate, the King of kings and Lord of lords."

What is here said may be understood either of God the Father, who shall at the last day manifest His glory to the world, or of Christ Himself, who shall then manifest His own glory. But whether the Father or Son is here spoken of, the words are to be understood of God as a title properly belonging to the divine Being; for if they are here ascribed to Christ, 'tis especially on the account of His divine glory, or that glory He has as a divine Person.

There are three things that may be observed in what is here said of God:

1. The title given Him, that is, Potentate, which denotes the supreme power and dominion of God. The apostle in the context has reference to the persecutions that the churches suffered under earthly rulers or potentates, and particularly under Nero, the Roman Emperor who reigned about the time that Paul is supposed to have written this epistle. The Roman emperors were the greatest earthly potentates who ever reigned on earth.

The Roman Empire included most of the known world, and was much greater than any of those three monarchies that were before it, the Babylonian, Persian, or Grecian. Christ had suffered under one of these Roman emperors, Tiberius Caesar. He was put to death by Pontius Pilate, who was governor under Caesar. So mean and low did He appear at His first coming, so far from appearing in the glory of a potentate, that He was crucified as a slave. But at His second appearing He shall appear in a very different manner from what He did then. He shall then appear not as a slave, but as a glorious Prince, a mighty King, and as it is said in the following words: "King of kings and Lord of lords."

This was to encourage Timothy to be faithful, though he was persecuted by Nero, who was a very cruel prince, who raised the first general persecution against the Christian churches, that when Christ comes He whom he served in the ministry would appear as a great Potentate.

2. Here an attribute of this Potentate is mentioned, that is, blessedness or happiness. The word in the original properly signifies "happy."

3. We may observe here that God is distinguished in this glory. He is alone in it. He is the blessed and only Potentate, or the only blessed Potentate. In other words, His dominion, glory, and blessedness are so much above that of all other beings that He is, as it were, alone in dominion and blessedness. His power and dominion are so much above that of all other potentates that their dominion and power are as nothing in comparison to it. So He is, as it were, the only Potentate, and it is as though there were none other but He; for He is King over kings and Lord over lords. Nero and the other Roman emperors are as nothing to Him. Their power and dominion fall so much

short of His that they are nothing in comparison, and so He only is the blessed Potentate.

This term of appropriation or singularity belongs both to this title of Potentate and the attribute of blessedness; for as He is infinitely above all in power and dominion, so He is in His happiness. Though Christ appeared as a poor, afflicted, crucified man at His first appearing, as though none was so afflicted as He, yet at His second coming He will appear so much above all in glory and blessedness that it will appear as though He only was happy and blessed. The happiness of others is not nearly to be mentioned, and is as nothing in comparison to it because finite is nothing and bears no proportion to infinite.

DOCTRINE: God is a Being possessed of the most absolutely perfect happiness.

It is in this respect that He only is happy, or reigns in happiness alone. So God in Scripture is often said to be thus or thus, and to be possessed of these and these perfections alone, as though none other had any such thing, when the meaning is that He alone is possessed of them in an absolutely perfect manner. So it is said that He only is holy (Revelation 15:4), when the meaning is not that no other being has any holiness in comparison to Him, but that He only is holy with an absolutely perfect holiness, and that He, being infinitely above all others in holiness, is as much alone in this holiness as though there were no other being that had any but He, because finite bears no proportion to infinite.

So 'tis said in the next verse following that "He only hath immortality," when the meaning is not that no other beings are in any sense immortal, for men's souls are immortal; the angels are immortal; the saints have a blessed immortality and are those spoken of in Romans 2:7: "To them who by patient continuance in well doing seek for glory and honor and immortality, eternal life." So concerning the goodness of God, Christ says that there is none good but one, and that is God (Matthew 19:17). So of wisdom, He is called "the only wise God" (1 Timothy 1:17). Concerning the being of God, God has being in absolute perfection, and therein in an infinitely higher manner than any other being. And therefore the Scripture speaks as though there were no other who had any being but He, and 'tis said that He is and there is none else.

In handling this subject I would:

1. Show what is meant by happiness, and wherein it consists.
2. Show what is meant by God's being possessed of absolutely perfect happiness.
3. Offer some arguments to prove that God is possessed of such happiness.
4. Observe what the Scripture reveals of the manner in which God enjoys such happiness.

1. I would briefly show what happiness is and wherein it consists. Happiness is that rest and delight that an intelligent being has in the absence of evil and in the possession of its proper good. Happiness is opposite the presence of evil, for happiness can't consist with its contrary. The presence of evil brings suffering and misery, not happiness. But in order to have happiness there is required not only the absence of all evil—for happiness is not merely the absence of a negative thing—but something positive. If only

the absence of all evil without the enjoyment of any positive good were sufficient for happiness, then the stones and other insensible things that sense no evil may be said to be happy, or at least intelligent, being in a deep sleep and perfectly insensible of good or evil. The mere absence of all evil without the enjoyment of any good brings no one to happiness, but rather to nonentity or not being; for that which has no being suffers no evil nor enjoys any good.

In order to true happiness of any being, the good that is enjoyed must not be only apparent good, but it must be real good, and must be its proper good, the good which is suited and adopted to its nature. If there is not a full agreement between the good enjoyed and the nature of the being enjoying [that good], there can't be true happiness, for that can't be true rest. And happiness consists in that rest and pleasure that a being has in the absence of evil and the enjoyment of its proper good. The intelligent being that is in such a state is at rest.

Restlessness rises from two causes, either from suffering evil or the wont of needed good. The suffering of evil distresses the being that suffers, and so does the absence of needed good; for while that good is wonting, there will be an unsatisfied craving of nature after something to fill up the vacancy, to fill up the capacity and to satisfy the soul. But when this good is enjoyed, it confers rest; it gives pleasure and delight. And no other pleasure that anyone has can be said to be happiness but that which arises from the enjoyment of his proper good, that which is adapted to his nature.

And no rest or pleasure can be called happiness or blessedness but that which is enjoyed by intelligent beings. The brute creatures that have external sense, but are void of intellect or a faculty of understanding, are not capable of happiness; they may be free from evil, and also may enjoy their own proper good, and so may be said to have rest and pleasure, but not happiness. They are not properly blessed ones; they are not capable of this because they, being without a faculty of understanding, are not capable of the intelligent enjoyment of any good at all.

In order to happiness two things are requisite: an objective and a subjective good. The objective good is the object that is enjoyed, that in the beholding, possessing, and enjoying of which the being that enjoys them is happy. The subjective good is the excellency and pleasure of the being himself who enjoys the object; for if there is never so excellent an object possessed, yet there can be no happiness unless the being who possesses it is in a state of such perfection as to be in the best capacity to enjoy that good. 'Tis from the union of the subject and object, and their agreeing together, that happiness arises; but unless the subject is fitted, there will be no harmony—and so no happiness will arise from the union of the subject and the object.

In order to happiness there must be both an object and a faculty, and both must be good and fitted one to another, and united together. However excellent the object is, yet, if the faculty is not also excellent and in a perfect state, if the understanding isn't clear so as to perceive the good of the object, and if the will isn't in a right frame to choose it, to rest and rejoice in it, there can be no happiness.

Both the objective and subjective good wherein the happiness of God consists are within Himself. The object that is the good He enjoys is Himself. The beauty and loveliness of this object in beholding which He is happy is of Himself. The beauty is not received from any other, and that perfection of understanding and will whereby He perfectly sees and enjoys this object in this beauty He has is not from any other; no other has given Him light to discover this object to Him, or has sanctified His heart or imparted holiness to Him to cause Him to love and choose it, and to dispose Him to delight in it.

He is in all respects sufficient; there are infinite riches, an inexhaustible treasure and supply for that infinite happiness of God. But He has the infinite riches in Himself. He receives nothing, no, not the least thing from any other. This may suffice for a meaning of the nature of happiness in general.

2. I proceed now in the second place to show what is meant by God's being possessed of that happiness that is absolutely perfect. In order to this it must first be observed that there is a twofold perfection of happiness.

First, there is that by which creatures are said to be perfectly happy according to their kind and capacity. Thus the saints and angels in heaven are said to be perfectly happy. But it is not with a universal absolute perfection. But it is their kind of perfection, consisting in a perfect answerableness to their nature, their rank and place, their particular good, and the particular measure of their capacity whereby they are perfectly free from all evil, and have the enjoyment of as much good as they desire and are capable of; they are satisfied and filled with happiness.

But this is perfection only of a certain kind, a limited perfection consistent with a manifold imperfection. Indeed, their capacity is filled, but their capacity itself is imperfect and very small; they are capable of but little. They have happiness proportioned to their understandings, but their understandings have infinite imperfection; for there is infinitely more that they don't know than that they do. By reason of this imperfection, it is said in Job 4:18: "His angels He hath charged with folly." This perfection is only perfection of a certain kind and capacity, which perfection admits of many degrees. There may be many, all of whom may be perfect in their kind, and yet one falling very short of another as being imperfect in comparison to another.

But, second, there is an absolute and unlimited perfection of happiness that is not a perfection of a certain particular kind, but a universal perfection, comprehending the utmost perfection, or all possible perfection. And therefore such perfection as admits of no degrees and no kind of limits is perfect in every way, excludes everything that may in any respect whatsoever be said to be imperfection.

And God is perfectly happy with such a perfection as this inasmuch as He is infinitely happy. A finite happiness can't be absolutely perfect because the limitation it has is an imperfection. But God is happy without any limitation. His delight and joy is not only inconceivably great, as being beyond any bounds that our thoughts can extend to, but 'tis really and properly so great as to be without any bounds. He enjoys pleasure that is infinitely sweet. The happiness of the most glorious and blessed saint or angel in heaven is but a small drop, but God's happiness is an infinite ocean. The pleasure that the saints and angels enjoy is indeed a sweet beam of light, but the pleasure God enjoys is a boundless fountain of light.

He is not only perfectly free of all evil, but infinitely distant from it and above it. He has not only happiness answerable to His capacity, but that capacity is infinite.

He is independently happy. 'Tis a thing that shows the imperfection of the most glorious and blessed of creatures, that their happiness is dependent; they are imperfect beings, and so are not self-sufficient, but are altogether insufficient for themselves and in themselves, and so are wholly depended for all their happiness. But God is not happy by deriving any good from any other. His happiness is not bestowed upon Him. He is not obliged to any for it. He is not dependent on their power or on their counsel and conduct or their love for any of His happiness. Nor does His happiness consist in the enjoyment of any other being beside Himself. His happiness is not complex or made up of many different kinds of enjoyments, or the enjoyment of various objects and various kinds of good, or that which comes partly in one way and partly in another way.

But His happiness is but one; 'tis simple, uncompounded, and undivided. His infinite happiness is of Himself and in Himself. There is no external fountain whence He obtains His supplies; but the infinite fountain is within Himself alone; 'tis all originally there, having no external cause or rise, and is not from the enjoyment of any external object. He is His own object, His own infinite good.

Third, this happiness of God's is eternal. He is happy from eternity; as His being is, so is His happiness. He has no beginning. His happiness neither is nor ever was a new thing. 'Tis with all the happiness of creatures which shows its imperfection, as to be young argues imperfection. The happiness of the saints was preceded by misery. God bestows new light and new favor upon them whereby they have new happiness, such as they never experienced before; they are brought out of misery into happiness, and can say that they never knew what true joy and true peace were before. There was a time when the being (and so the happiness) of the angels was new, but God's happiness is from everlasting. No part of His happiness is new. His happiness was the same before the world was created, and so it is to everlasting. None can ever deprive Him of it. The glory of earthly kingdoms comes to an end; the glory of the visible world will cease; the brightness of the sun that has continued for so many ages will vanish away—but the happiness of God never will come to an end. And therefore He is said to be blessed forevermore. 2 Corinthians 11:31: "The God and Father of our Lord Jesus Christ, which is blessed for evermore." The happiness of all creatures is in its own nature liable to come to an end, and angels fall.

Fourth, God is unchangeably happy, which is another thing wherein the absolute perfection of His happiness consists. It is not liable to ebbs and flows; 'tis not sometimes increased by any new discoveries. It has no intermissions or abatements, but ever remains the same. This Father of lights, this Fountain of light ever has the same individual and infinite brightness, without the least variableness or shadow of turning.

It was the same after man rebelled against Him as it was before. It is the same since the angels sinned and turned devils, and hate Him and blaspheme Him and set themselves against Him as it was before while they loved Him and praised Him; it is never diminished, neither is it ever added to.

3. I now proceed in the third place to show that God is possessed of such an absolutely perfect happiness. And the consideration of what has been said already of the nature of happiness will make this evident if we consider, first, that the glory and beauty of the divine nature are infinite. He must be an infinite Being, because He is not from any other, but is necessarily of Himself. If He had any limits, these limits must be of some precise measure, no greater or smaller, and therefore must have had some cause to limit it. There must be some cause why He is so great and no greater; for one measure of limitation is certainly no more necessary in itself than another. And seeing that God is infinite, His understanding and power, and so all His perfections must be infinite; and therefore He has infinite glory and excellence.

Second, He must perfectly understand and behold His own infinite glory and beauty. To suppose Him to be infinitely perfect and to not perfectly know and view His own glory would imply a contradiction; for His being infinitely perfect supposes Him to be of infinite understanding. And therefore it must be that He beholds all His own glory perfectly and has a comprehensive view of His own infinite beauty and loveliness. And therefore, if God delights to behold that which is beautiful, and loves to see that which is lovely, it must necessarily follow that His delight in beholding His own beauty must be infinite.

If the creature is made so exceedingly happy in seeing but little of the glory of God, then He must be infinitely more happy who sees infinitely more of it. He who loves to behold beauty must have pleasure in proportion to the degree of beauty that He beholds; and therefore, if He perfectly beholds and fully comprehends that beauty and glory which is infinite, His pleasure must be infinite.

The capacity is infinite by the supposition, because He is of infinite understanding; and the objective good is infinite because the beauty understood is infinite. And therefore the good is equal to the capacity, and consequently is sufficient to fill it. But an infinite capacity filled up with happiness must contain infinite happiness.

Third, God must necessarily perfectly love His own beauty and excellency. To suppose Him to be infinitely excellent, and not perfectly to love His excellency would be a contradiction; for 'tis wont of excellency not to love excellency—and that is a great defect.

So, then, 'tis necessary that God's delight in His own infinite beauty should be in proportion to His understanding of it; and therefore His acquiescence in it must be infinite. God has both infinite objective good and also infinite subjective good in Himself, and an infinite capacity. He has infinite objective good as He has infinite beauty to behold, and He has infinite capacity or infinite knowledge to behold this infinite beauty. He has infinite subjective good, as He has infinite holiness to love and delight in His own beauty and excellency. And therefore nothing can be lacking in order to His being infinitely happy.

And seeing that He has this capacity and this objective and subjective good in and of Himself from eternity, and unchangeably, hence it must follow that He has this infinite happiness in an absolute independence, eternity, and immutability. And so His happiness is in all respects absolutely perfect.

Fourth, He is the Fountain of all happiness. All the objective good and all the inherent good that is in the world are from Him. He is the Father of lights from whence comes every good and perfect gift (James 1:17). All the beauty and excellency in which anyone is delighted, all the understanding and sight to behold them, and all the disposition in the heart to love them must be from Him, for He is the First Cause, and all others have their very being from Him. And shall not God have that Himself which He gives to others? Yea, shall not the Fountain be inexhaustible that continually does and forever will send for such to fill heaven and earth without weariness and diminution of itself?

Lastly, God must be infinitely above all that should hurt Him, for He, being of Himself without any cause, must be independent. And seeing that all things are from Him, and all their power, 'tis impossible, and implies a contradiction to suppose that He is in any measure dependent on their power. For what an absurdity it is that that their power should objectively be dependent on Him, and that all should be from Him, and yet in some respect He be dependent on their power. And He being Himself infinite in power must be infinitely above the reach of any, because

He must have all other beings in His hands, to do with them as He pleases—and therefore He must be independently and immutably happy.

4. I come now to the fourth and last thing purposed in the doctrinal handling of this subject, and that is to take notice of what the Scripture reveals of the manner. 'Tis impossible for us to conceive of the particular manner in which God enjoys Himself, rejoices in Himself, and so has infinite acquiescence and delight in Himself. God is infinitely above us, and His glory and blessedness are infinitely above the reach of our thoughts. We are told even with respect to the future glory of the saints themselves that eye has not seen nor ear heard of all that God has for them that love Him. And if the saints' happiness in God is so much above our conceptions, how much more must the infinite blessedness of God Himself be above the conceptions of the saints and angels in heaven?

Yet we may know something from what God has revealed in the Scriptures, partly from what God teaches us of His image, and partly from what He reveals of His essence, and partly from what He reveals of His subsistence in the Persons of the Trinity.

1. We may learn something by what the Scripture reveals of His image in the saints, inasmuch as the Scripture reveals the holy rest and joy that the saints have to be an image and communication of the happiness of God; for the Scripture reveals that the saints, in their spiritual enjoyments that they enjoy, have fellowship with God Himself. 1 John 1:3: "That which we have seen and heard declare we unto you, that ye also may have fellowship with us. And truly our fellowship is with the Father, and with His

Son, Jesus Christ." By the word "fellowship" here is signified and intended a common partaking with others. When the apostle says, "that ye may have fellowship with us," he means also to have fellowship with the Father and His son Jesus Christ. So the word "fellowship" is always used in Scripture for a partaking in some thing in common with some others. So we learn that the saints, in that special happiness that they enjoy, partake of God's happiness, or of the happiness of the Father and His Son Jesus Christ in their measure and manner. In those spiritual pleasures they enjoy, they partake of God's pleasures; they enjoy something of God's light, as the psalmist says in Psalm 36:8: "Thou shall make them to drink of the river of Thy pleasures." So that in the holy pleasures they have, they do, as it were, taste of God's own pleasures.

And so it follows in verse 9: "In Thy light shall we see light." So by this may be learned something of the nature of that infinite pleasure and happiness that God enjoys; for this shows that though it is infinitely above all that we know of or can conceive of, yet the holy pleasure of the saints is the image of it, and the most like it of any kind of happiness and pleasure. He who has had the experience of this sort of pleasure knows more of God than it is possible for others to know, and may, by considering the nature of his own holy delight and joy, know something of the nature of God's happiness and joy in Himself. Though he can know infinitely little of it, yet he can know more than others; as a little taste, though it is but a little, will give a more clear idea of any kind of pleasure than anything else can.

2. We may know something by what the Scripture reveals of the essence of God, particularly in that the Scripture teaches us that God is light and love. It teaches that
God is light, as in 1 John 1:5. And so it teaches that He is
love (1 John 4:8).

In these things we have declared that wherein God's
happiness consists, for reason and experience teaches that
these two things necessarily fill a mind with pleasure and
joy. Light is sweet, especially spiritual divine light; it rejoices
the heart, and if there is infinite light in God, without any
darkness at all, there will be infinite blessedness in Him
without any sorrow at all. Love is a sweet affection or principle, and if it is not crossed, but the beloved object is fully
enjoyed, it is a spring of delight and pleasure. The apostle
teaches that unspeakable joy rises in the hearts of the
saints from light and love. 1 Peter 1:8: "Whom having not
seen ye love, in whom though now ye see Him not, yet believing ye rejoice with joy unspeakable and full of glory."
Hence we learn that the infinite blessedness of God arises
from His infinite light and love.

3. We learn something from what the Scripture teaches
us concerning the sacred Trinity. In the Scripture is expressed that God the Deity is happy in the communion
and mutual enjoyment there is between the Persons of the
Trinity. The Scripture teaches us that God the Father and
God the Son have eternal delight, happiness, and joy one
in another, as you may see in Proverbs 8:30: "Then was I by
him as one brought up with him, and I was daily his delight, rejoicing always before him." Here we are expressly
told that God the Son is the eternal delight of the Father,
or that object in the enjoyment of which the Father's infi-

nite and eternal delight and happiness consists. So the happiness of God the Father consists in the enjoyment of His only begotten and duly-beloved Son. So also this place expressly teaches us that God the Son has His joy and rejoicing in the Father in those words, "rejoicing always before Him."

Christ speaks of the glory that He had, as He was God from eternity, as consisting in fellowship with the Father, and the Father's glory as consisting in fellowship with Him in those words that He says to the Father in John 17:5: "And now, Holy Father, glorify Me with Thine own self, with the glory I had with Thee before the world was." So this teaches us how God is love, and wherein the infinite, essential love of God particularly consists, that is, in that love there is between the Father and the Son. It is doubtless with respect to this love especially that God is said to be love; this love is infinitely transcendent above all the love of God to creatures, and is the fountain of all other love of God.

And this, above all other things, tends to give us an idea how God is happy in the enjoyment of Himself. The happiness of God is but one and comes but one way. There is not a twofold infinite happiness in the Deity, that comes partly one way and partly in another. Such would make it complex and imperfect, like the joy of the creature. And the Scripture is express that God's joy comes this way, that is, by the communion of the Persons of the blessed Trinity. The happiness of God seems to consist in an infinitely pure, perfect, and eternal act of love and joy between the Father and the Son, wherein the Deity, as it were, wholly flows out in a spirit of infinite love and delight, proceeding from both the Father and the Son.

God is happy in beholding the brightness of His own glory; but this glory He beholds in beholding His Son, whom, we are told, is the brightness of His glory, the express image of His Person (Hebrews 1:3). In beholding this perfect, express image, He has an infinitely more perfect view of Himself and the brightness of His own glory than a man has who beholds his own image in a glass. And thus it is that God loves and delights in Himself, in that infinite and eternal delight that is between the Father and the Son. And because God's happiness thus consists in the communion of the Persons of the Trinity, and the love and delight of the Father and the Son in each other, hence the apostle, when speaking of the special happiness of Christians, and how that therein they partake of the happiness of God, mentions the Persons of the Trinity and says, "Our fellowship is with the Father, and with His Son Jesus Christ."

Application

USE OF INSTRUCTION. This use will be in several inferences:

1. From hence we may learn God's holiness and righteousness, all from some independent pleasure or delight.

2. From this absolutely, perfect happiness of God we may see the glory of the goodness of God. In God's being infinitely happy he enjoys infinite goodness in Himself; in His being ready to communicate His happiness He is good

to others. The goodness of God is, as it were, the overflowing of that infinite fountain of good that is in the Deity; and all the good things that the creature enjoys are streams from that fountain. This shows the freeness of God's goodness in all the instances of it. The freeness of God's goodness is the glory of it in that God is infinitely happy in Himself.

It will follow that God never bestows any good thing on any creature from any obligation that ever He has been laid under to the creature. No creature has ever obliged Him by doing Him any good, by affording Him any help in any distress or difficulty or suffering; for He never was nor ever could be under any difficulty or suffering, being infinitely above it. No creature ever obliged Him by assisting Him to accomplish anything that was too great for His strength alone; for He is almighty, and all strength is from Him. No creature ever obliged Him by giving Him any counsel in any difficult or intricate case; for He who is infinitely happy is self-sufficient. His power and happiness are sufficient for His own designs and purposes. And therefore the apostle cries out as he does in Romans 11:33–36: "Oh, the depth of the riches both of the wisdom and knowledge of God! How unsearchable are His judgments, and His ways past finding out! For who hath known the mind of the Lord? Or who hath been His counselor? Or who hath first given to Him, and it shall be recompensed unto him again? For of Him, and through Him, and to Him are all things, to whom be glory forever."

None ever obliged God by giving Him anything He needed, for He never stood in need of anything, for He is perfectly and infinitely happy in Himself. He never needed anything; none ever obliged Him by bestowing any present on Him to add to His dignity and glory, no jewel to adorn His crown, or to add to the convenience and pleasantness of His life; for He is infinitely above the reach of our presents. His happiness is infinitely above any addition from us. Psalm 16:2: "O my soul, thou hast said unto the Lord, Thou art my Lord; my goodness extendeth not to Thee."

None ever obliged God by helping to defend Him from any danger, for by His eternal, immutable happiness He is in Himself infinitely above all danger. A son may in many things help a father, relieve him under difficulties, defend him from dangers, and add to the comfort of his life. A subject may oblige a great prince; he may do a great deal for him; he may relieve him in distress; he may fight for him and defend him by his sword, and may save his life; he may help to extend his dominion and may advance his honor and dignity; he may contribute to his riches. But none can oblige by helping that blessed and only Potentate that we read of in the text. By all our love and all our service He receives nothing at our hands. Job 22:2–4: "Can a man be profitable unto God, as he that is wise may be profitable unto himself? Is it any pleasure to the Almighty that thou art righteous? Or is it gain to Him that thou makest thy way perfect? Will He reprove thee for fear of Thee? Will He enter with thee into judgment?" And chapter 35:6–7: "If thou be righteous, what givest thou Him or what receiveth He of thine hand?" Psalm 50:12: "If I were hungry, I would not tell thee."

From the absolutely perfect and immutable happiness of God, it will follow that God never bestows any good thing on any creature from fear of him. Men oftentimes show kindness to others so that they may not do 'em any hurt; they are afraid of their displeasure, and therefore are willing to make 'em friendly for their own interest. Yea, policy has often sought the greatest and most powerful princes or earthly potentates to show kindness to some particular subjects who were men of strength and influence so that they might be attached to their interest, and lest they should make some disturbance and difficulty. Most earthly princes find themselves obliged to condescend in many things to their subjects for fear of them, lest they should rebel against them.

But by the doctrine we may learn that God never bestows any kindness out of fear of anyone; for He, being immutably and infinitely happy, is above their reach. Job 22:4: "Will he reprove thee for fear of thee? Will He enter with thee into judgment?" Job 35:6–8: "If thou sinnest, what doest thou against Him? Or if thy transgressions be multiplied, what doest thou unto Him? If thou be righteous, what givest thou Him or what receiveth He of thine hand? Thy wickedness may hurt a man as thou art; and thy righteousness may profit the son of man."

Nothing is more common in earthly kingdoms than for princes to spare rebels or traitors, and show 'em a great deal of leniency when they deserve to die out of prudence and for reasons of state. It may be that they will put some to death but spare others, lest the people should be exasperated, and tumults should be made. But God never spares a rebel or traitor on any such account, for the rage and tumults of men and devils can do Him no hurt. 'Tis in vain for them to set themselves against Him in battle, as much as for a parcel of dry briars and thorns to set themselves in battle array with their points forward against flames of devouring fire. Isaiah 27:4: "Fury is not in Me; who would set the briers and thorns against Me in battle? I would go through them. I would burn them together."

3. This doctrine shows that God never shows anyone any kindness out of any hope or expectation of any recompense. He doesn't show kindness as men often do, in hope of receiving as much again, or of ever getting anything by it; for He who is already infinitely rich and happy can't gain anything.

This freeness and excellency of God's goodness to us calls for our praises. We ought to consider this when we taste the fruits of God's bounty to us, that these things are bestowed upon us out of the sovereign riches of God's grace, without our having ever obliged Him by anything we have done to profit Him, and from one to whom we cannot do any hurt, and who never has any expectation that we ever shall requite Him or be any profit to Him.

Hence learn how greatly the love and kindness of God differs from our love and kindness. As God's happiness is infinite and independent, so His goodness is independent; it has its rise, ground, and motive wholly within Himself. It can't be otherwise with an independent, self-sufficient Being, and one of absolutely perfect happiness. Hence the apostle speaks of the kindness of God in one instance, and in elsewhere so often uses that expression "according to His good pleasure," or "according to the good pleasure of His will." Luke 12:32: "It is the Father's good pleasure to give you the kingdom." Ephesians 1:5: "Having predestinated us according to His good pleasure." Philippians 2:13: "Both to will and to do of His good pleasure."

2 Thessalonians 1:11: "That God would fulfill in you all the good pleasure of His goodness."

But man's kindness and love are dependent; they have their cause, fountain, ground, motive, and goodness outside of himself. And therefore God's love is free in a sense that no other love is. The goodness of God is universally and absolutely free, which can't be said of any other goodness.

But more particularly, let us consider:

1. How God's love to us differs from our love to God. Our love to God is given to us by God, and is the fruit of His love to us; but God's love to us is originally from Himself. If God had not first loved us and, as a fruit of His love had not inserted a principle of love into us, we never would have loved Him. Our love to God is a great gift, and a fruit of infinite kindness; but God needed not to have love inserted into His heart for those whom He loves; it was there from eternity, and was of Himself.

2. Men are first stirred up to seek the love of God in their hearts by the fear of God's displeasure. They are at first at enmity against God, and have the startings of God's wrath for it, and hence are stirred up to seek to have a change wrought in their hearts, though they are very opposed to it. Fear drives 'em to it, and they are, as it were, forced and driven to it against their inclination; for if God did not threaten 'em they would forever rise only in their hatred of God. They would have full complacence in their own hatred, which shows that our love to God is not from that kind of freedom and self-origination that the love of God is from.

3. When men do love God, their love is attracted by the loveliness of God, but God's love sees nothing in us to attract it, but flows out of itself; for God set His love upon us out of mere goodness when He beheld us without any loveliness (Ezekiel 16:6–8). Hence God is said to love His people because He loves them. Deuteronomy 7:7–8: "The Lord did not set His love upon you, nor choose you, because ye were more in number than any people, for ye were the fewest of all people, but because the Lord loved you."

4. Our love to God is for His worthiness and is infinitely less than His worthiness; but God loves us without worthiness. He loves you with your infinite unworthiness. Our love is not only attracted and drawn by God's worthiness of our love, but after all it is infinitely short of any equality to the loveliness of the being beloved. But God's love is not only not attracted by any loveliness in us to attract it; but it overcame infinite repulsion. When He saw nothing but hatefulness in us, infinite hatefulness, yet He loved us.

5. We love God because He has won us by His love and kindness to us, whereas His love has no motive out of Himself. God's love is not only the cause that gave our love to God, but 'tis the good or motive of it. 1 John 4:19: "We love Him because He first loved us." We never showed any kindness to God to win His love; for He that is infinitely happy is above our kindness. But God has shown infinite kindness to sinful men to win their love.

6. We don't love God without an expectation of infinite benefit by Him, whereas God loves us without expectation or possibility of any benefit by us. When a godly man sets his love on God, it is as all his happiness and as his

Chief Good, because he sees Him to be the Fountain of happiness, the only happiness fit for him and sufficient for him. But God's happiness doesn't consist in man, but in Himself, which shows how infinitely more disinterested God's love to man is than is man's love to God. And besides, man has many precious and glorious promises of reward and eternal blessedness to encourage his love to God.

God has promised to eternally reward him for it. He has promised a crown of life to them who love Him (James 1:12). He has promised to give Himself to them for their everlasting portion and to make them blessed forever.

But God loves us without any expectation of anything from us to reward Him, for He cannot be rewarded, being infinitely happy in Himself. What cause we have therefore to praise God for His grace and love toward us, to admire it and give all glory to Him whose love for us is in so many respects infinitely above all our love for Him.

God is not only then above the love of sinful men, but infinitely above the love of the brightest and most glorious angel of heaven; for their love for God is given of God. It has all its foundation and motive in God, and not in themselves. They love God because He first loved them; they love Him for His worthiness; and their love falls infinitely short of an equality with that worthiness. Their love is attracted by God's love, and their love is infinitely to their interest; for all their happiness is in the being they love, and their love is infinitely rewarded by Him—whereas His love for them is absolutely free and disinterested. 'Tis not a gift of anyone. His benevolence is not attracted to them, and His love has no motive outside Himself.

Let it be considered how God's kindness to us differs from our kindness one to another. First, it is infinitely greater. How little love have we in our hearts?

Second, any true love for our fellow creatures is given of God. Men have offended us, yet we have the expectation of them doing us good. Men are encouraged by rewards.

Hence we learn the wonderfulness of the love of Christ, that one who was infinitely and eternally happy should become miserable for us so that we who are miserable may be happy.

He is eternally happy. He is one who is possessed of all that happiness that has been spoken of. So He is absolutely, perfectly, independently, eternally, infinitely, and unchangeably happy. Thus happy is He in the love of the Father, and in the enjoyment of His love. He is said to be God blessed forevermore (Romans 9:5).

He became man, and so a weak, dependent creature, dependent on God for happiness, subject to God in the form of a servant, a poor, afflicted man, a man of sorrows.

How wonderful a sight was this, to see Him who was light, and in whom was no darkness at all, veiled and covered with such darkness. The infinite Fountain of Life became subject to death. God blessed forevermore was made a curse. The Fountain of infinite delight and joy felt pain. The brightness of God's glory suffered ignominy. He who was the infinite delight of the Father suffered the infinite wrath of the Father so that we who are miserable might be happy, that He might bring we who are most deservedly miserable to that great Fountain of blessedness. He did this so that we might have fellowship with the Father and with His Son, that we might be made to drink of the river of God's pleasures.

What cause have we to admire, to praise and extol the Lord Jesus Christ, and to praise God for this unspeakable gift, and for all the blessings we receive through Him. What can have a greater tendency to excite us to thankfulness for our mercies than to think that they are procured for us by this means, by His becoming miserable.

If it is so that God is possessed of infinite blessedness, how happy are the saints who have fellowship with Him, who are brought to such a union with God as in their manner and measure to be partakers of the same happiness, to drink of the same fountain or river of pleasure. So do all the saints in a degree in all that spiritual comfort, peace, and joy they have in this world. And then they are entitled to the more full and perfect fellowship with God in His heavenly kingdom and glory in His presence where is fullness of joy and at His right hand where are pleasures forevermore, where they shall be as vessels that are thrown into that infinite ocean of pleasure which God is possessed of, to partake with God of it and have as much of it as they can hold. What blessed and happy persons therefore are the saints with whom it is this way!

USE OF EXAMINATION. This doctrine may put persons who think themselves godly upon examining themselves with respect to two things:

1. Whether or not they have a spirit to rejoice in the happiness of God. This is a proper trait whether we have a love of benevolence towards God. They who have a true love for God have both a love of benevolence and complacency. A love of benevolence seeks and delights in the

happiness of another; complacence delights in beholding and enjoying the beauty and love of another. A love of benevolence to those who are capable of having happiness added to them appears in seeking their good.

But God, being infinitely happy, we can't add to His happiness. But the same love that seeks that good which the object of love does not have rejoices. Therefore they who have a true benevolence to God have a spirit to rejoice; it is a pleasant theme to them when they hear how happy God is. They rejoice that God is infinitely happy because He appears worthy of it to them. Love for Him disposes them to acquiesce in His blessedness.

2. Whether you have a spirit to choose God as the Fountain of your happiness. God, being possessed of an absolutely perfect blessedness is the Fountain of all happiness. From this infinite Fount are all streams, and in God's light alone can we see true light. Have you a spirit therefore to choose God? Every man loves happiness and is in pursuit of it. Does your heart tend that way for happiness? This is the proper kind of love of complacence.

How wonderful is it that God will accept our praises, for we learn by the doctrine that they do not add the least to His happiness. Neither love and praises of heart, nor praises of the lips, nor praises in life add anything to His infinite blessedness. When the saints' hearts are enlarged, God receives nothing.

God has a multitude of glorious angels, thousands and thousands continuously praising Him. God is infinitely above them. The praises of these glorious spirits rise very high, to a height that is inconceivable by us; but God's happiness is infinitely above this height. God stoops infinitely to behold the things that are done in heaven. That infinite light doesn't shine the brighter. The infinite joy is not in the least increased; it does but remain the same unaltered light that it was infinite ages before the angels had any being, and before the creation of the world.

The blessed and only Potentate does but reign in the same calm, perfect, and unaltered blessedness that is infinitely above not only the praises, but all the thoughts and conceptions of the glorious angels. Not one of the angels alone, nor all together, can by their love and praise reach up to God so as to add one beam to that infinite brightness, or one drop to that infinite blessedness.

How wonderful then is it that God will accept such praises as we offer to Him, that are so vastly below those of the angels, who are but poor babes in comparison of them. Yet God is pleased out of the mouth of babes to ordain and accept praise. We are but worms of the dust. How low, heavy, and dull are our best and most fervent praises in comparison to theirs. And how much sinful imperfection, how much coldness, how much vile and shameful hypocrisy, how little fervency, how little sincerity at best, how much loathsome pollution with that little spirit of sincerity—and yet if there be the least sincerity, God appears ready to accept our praises. How wonderful is His condescension and grace in it, and how should the consideration of it engage our hearts to be more fervent in His praises.